Secrets of a Stingy Scoundrel

100 Dirty Little Money-Grubbing Secrets

PHIL VILLARREAL

Illustrations by Adam Wallenta

Skyhorse Publishing

Skyhorse Publishing books may be purchased in bulk at special discounts for sales promotion, corporate gifts, fund-raising, or educational purposes. Special editions can also be created to specifications. For details, contact the Special Sales Department, Skyhorse Publishing, 555 Eighth Avenue, Suite 903, New York, NY 10018 or info@skyhorsepublishing.com.

www.skyhorsepublishing.com

10 9 8 7 6 5 4 3 2 1

Library of Congress Cataloging-in-Publication Data

Villarreal, Phil.
  Secrets of a stingy scoundrel : 100 dirty little money-grubbing secrets / by Phil Villarreal.
      p. cm.
ISBN 978-1-60239-754-5 (pbk. : alk. paper)
1. Finance, Personal--Humor. 2. Budgets, Personal--Humor.
3. Money--Humor. I. Title.

    PN6231.F47V55 2009
814'.6--dc22
                              2009015335

Printed in China

For Luke and Emma.

Contents

Threeword
(Because I'm Too Stingy for a Foreword)

Honor. Integrity. Honesty. Dignity.

If you live by any of these values, you may as well drop the book right now, because they're against everything it professes. All are pricey conveniences that don't give you a decent return on your investment.

When philosophizing in terms of money, it's always best to think like a robot, separating yourself from emotion and sensitivity in order to optimize each situation for maximum savings potential. If that doesn't work for you, then try behaving as a celebrity, imagining yourself as someone to whom society's rules don't apply. Walk around with an arrogant conviction that you're better than everyone and don't deserve to pay the same amount as others.

The following pages contain my lifelong accumulation of cash-sparing tactics. Read on and you will be schooled in the black arts of scoundrel-ism. You'll discover cons, ruses, and sleights of hand that will dazzle your opponents, which are often corporations that stack the deck against those who aren't aware of the secrets of subversion.

My advice does contain a few splashes of innovation, but much of it is simple common sense, often stretched beyond reason to the deranged extreme. Surely many of my ideas have occurred to you at some point, only to be abruptly scuttled by your inner decency filter. Lucky for you, I've taken my filter off to allow you full benefit of my chicanery.

Contained herein is practical, tried advice that will allow you to stoop to depths you might have never thought possible in order to stop being screwed out of money, and in some cases make a few extra bucks. I've written brief essays on each of the suggestions, incorporating examples, rationales, and potential pitfalls for all of them. These tips are divided into eight general sections for quick reference. I've saved the gnarliest stuff, which is more for humor's sake than practicality, for section nine.

If you choose to apply some of my tips to your own lifestyle, do so with discretion; also know that you'll possibly be facing dirty looks, slaps in the face, disapproving phone calls from parents, divorces, or, in some cases, confrontations with security guards or surly store managers. So above all, act with cunning. It's all about bending the rules without quite breaking them.

Disclaimer time: Don't break any laws or get the impression that I'm advocating criminal behavior because this book was written for entertainment purposes. Look both ways before you put out fires and stop, drop, and roll before you cross the street and all that.

Much of what I write will surely disgust you, but I'm sure a sizable portion is intriguing and perhaps you'll incorporate a few of my tokens into your daily routine. Come now, and make a dollar outta 15 cents with me.

Personal

This section covers what you wear, how you groom yourself, and how to make a wart disappear through an ancient practice known as sticking duct tape on it. Not included are instructions on how to fold up pages of this book to make little hats for yourself, because that would be idiotic, and this book is all about being brilliant.

1. All the Free T-shirts, Hats, Squeeze Bottles, and Hip Sacks a Man Could Ever Want

If I were a truly great man, I'd be able to form my entire wardrobe solely out of free clothing I attained in return for signing up for credit cards. Alas, only a quarter of my closet consists of such garments.

Companies set up kiosks at college campuses, fairgrounds, and outside sporting events hoping to lure you into their clutches by offering a bevy of knickknacks. My favorite of these free gifts is the T-shirt. I could write poetry about how much I love them, but for fear of driving you away so early in the book, I'll abstain. Covering the top half of your body is only the beginning of their wonders. Shirts also double as carwash towels, dishcloths, flag football flags, spaghetti strainers, lampshades, and do-rags, just to name a few potential uses. They're magical, really. And they're generously donated by kindly organizations looking to fix it up so you can pay for things you need by sliding little plastic cards through innocuous machines.

The squeeze bottle, another popular giveaway at these booths, isn't quite so useful. I wouldn't recommend drinking out of it because of the plastic-y taste it inflicts on water contained within, but you'd be amazed how handy they are on road trips. The resealable pop-tops make for handy depositories for urine, saving your party multiple stops on the merry way to your destination.

It's a shame the hip sack, also known as a "fanny pack," is an indisputable symbol of dorkiness and is only acceptable attire for professional speed walkers and senior citizens on gambling expeditions, because it's so darn effective at stowing away your stuff. It takes a real man, the same type of guy who will wear a pink dress shirt, to proudly rock a fanny pack. Alas, my ego prevents me from wearing mine outside. If only I had enough

self-confidence to keep it on in public, maybe I could start a new trend.

Thankfully, society deems the wearing of any and all types of baseball caps as the pinnacle of hipness. Until the turn of the millennium, trucker hats weren't known as suitable headgear for anyone but mulleted, cargo transportation industry drivers, but thanks to the efforts of Ashton Kutcher and Paris Hilton, even those castaways regained their social relevance. The more obscure and corporately dominated your hat is, the more ironically cool you look for wearing it.

I'll admit that I've been carried away thus far about the benefits of taking free credit-card booth stuff and coy about addressing the potential harm in doing so. It's true that getting too many cards can drive down your credit score and it's doubly certain that most any card offered to the general public isn't worth acquiring due to its nasty interest rates and pitiful rewards.

You'll have to stand up to the booth staffers by refusing to fill out the clip-boarded paperwork that's supposed to be a prerequisite to getting the freebies. Many times, especially if it's late in the day, they'll acquiesce and give you what you want without demanding to reclaim your application. If the person standing between you and your *South Park* Cartman shirt happens to be a bastard stickler for the rules, kindly just fill out the form with an alias, and never include your real social security number. If they check your name on the form against an ID, transpose numbers on your address and fill out the zip code illegibly or a digit short to ensure you'll never get approved.

2. Watches Are the Devil

In the age of cell phones, watches are not only unnecessary, they're also downright vile. Your phone is automatically programmed to the second to sync with the official time bouncing from satellites. Since most people have cell phones and use them to tell the time, if you mis-synchronize your timepiece you'll end up looking like an idiot.

Another problem with watches is the way they retain soapy water whenever you wash your hands, causing them to fester underneath the band. Even if you happen to be skilled enough to wash without wetting the watch, you'll still have to put up with awkward tan lines. You just can't win with these things. Fasten them too loose and they slip up and down your wrist like the Times Square New Year's ball; pull them too tight and they leave irritating red marks.

Do not, by any means, ever buy or keep a watch. This is not negotiable. The darn things are little, wrist-affixed money pits, making you shell out for new batteries, new bands, and eventually full replacements. Wearing a watch can be habit-forming and could be a jewelry-gateway drug toward rings, gold chains, cuff links, and, *gulp*, man-purses.

Why certain backward, tradition-bound people of today still give watches out as gifts baffles me. Watch-giving is a clear sign of lunacy, as well as an aggressive act of cruelty. It's up to you to do your part to stand up to such violations of your trust by thanking the giver politely before jetting off to the retailer from whence it came to return it for store credit. If there's no gift receipt attached, hit up a pawnshop and give it away at the first price offered without negotiation, lest the shopkeeper change his mind, come to his senses, and refuse the item altogether. Do not pass this watch on to someone else as a present, thinking you're getting away with something, because even though you may not have purchased the watch, the act of giving it to someone else makes you as much of an ass as the person who gave it to you.

Should the giver ever accost you by asking you why you're not wearing your timepiece and wondering aloud whether you really liked it, say that it broke or you left it somewhere by accident. You'll be telling the truth, for it has broken your heart and it was truly an accident to leave it wherever you did, be it an exchange counter or pawnshop display case, instead of doing what a morally right person would have done and hurling it right back at the giver's face.

3. Straight from the Cauldron

The shame of this great nation is that witchdoctors, soothsayers, and healers no longer patrol our roadsides. They've been forced away by the cold, antiseptic HMO/health insurance complex, which is basically a legalized mafia that shakes down customers for ridiculous sums of protection money. I have no problem with mafias in theory—they exist to fill needs not provided by law-abiding society—but I am angry with the way the healthcare system stifles creativity and simplicity in medicine in favor of impersonality and maintaining the bottom line. Not only does the healthcare machine prevent the discovery of easy, cheap cures, it tries to get people to forget the knowledge of past generations.

In short, the doctor doesn't want you to know that duct tape takes away warts with just as much efficiency as an outpatient freeze-off procedure. Here are some more of my favorites.

- Coughs can be chased away with shots of hard liquor or, if you want to go a cheaper, less alcoholic route, by eating almonds, grapes, or onions.
- Garlic isn't only good for staving off vampires. It also stops jock itch cold. Hey, you never catch Mario or Luigi scratching their balls, do you?
- To soothe an earache, dab a cotton ball with olive oil, heat it up for a few seconds in a microwave, and then stick it in your ear. Also tasty with bread.

- Beat back nausea by downing a light, carbonated soft drink. The reason it works is that the bubbles magically make your tummy feel better.
- Momma always used to clean your mouth out with soap when you swore, but if she weren't so evil, she would have just made you eat up an onion. They make like Schwarzenegger with an AK-47 on all the bastard germs in your foul trap. Eat one a day and your toothache should disappear.
- Apples not only keep the doctor away but they also battle light depression with as much gusto as any prescription drug. Not poison apples, though. Those make you fall into a coma until dwarves resuscitate you and help you overthrow the jealous, evil queen who gave them to you.
- I don't know why, but whenever I have a headache and I eat Cinnamon Toast Crunch or its cheaper Malt-O-Meal cousin, Toasted Cinnamon Twists, it magically disappears. When I'm out of cereal, I just lay back and say a soothing word to myself over and over until the headache vanishes.

- If you want to get rid of your cold as quickly as possible, eat lemon slices. They're gross, but not as nasty as a constant stream of snot flowing out of your nose.
- If your toenails are cracked and discolored by fungus, pee on them. If you have difficulty urinating on yourself, dump mouthwash on your feet. But do not, I repeat, *do not* mix things up and pee inside your mouthwash container.
- It's tempting to cut corns off but doing so can lead to infection. A better way to erase them is to get a hold of some chalk, grind it up into a paste, and smear it around the bulges.

By the way, I pulled most of that stuff off the Internet in less than five minutes. Medical degree schmedical degree.

4. Self-styled

Worst: John Edwards spending $800 of his campaign money on a haircut.

Bad: My wife forking over $60 to get her hair "cut," meaning left exactly the same length and combed a little bit differently with a bunch of sweet-smelling gunk stuck in it.

Better: Me paying $12 to the place inside Wal-Mart for a crappy, uneven mop massacre.

Best: Cutting out the middle man and doing it yourself, or having it done by a friend or loved one whom you're reasonably sure won't carve a smiley face into the back of your head.

This last point is important, lest you go through life with the nickname "Smiley," like my college friend Smiley. The poor Canadian sap fell victim to the ruthless designs of my buddy Magill during sophomore year in the dorms. Smiley was looking to save a few bucks on a haircut just before a football game, and Magill allowed him to do exactly that, only with the unspoken corollary that Smiley, who would henceforth no longer be known as Dave, attends the game with a smiley face on the back of his head. He might still have the symbol to this day had a giggling group of freshman girls sitting behind us not pointed out the mishap to Smiley, who then made Magill shave his head completely. So long as Magill isn't your impromptu barber, you should be safe. But only the most sure-handed, patient, Mr. Miyagi–like among us is capable of taking a razor to his own head without getting Wal-Mart–like results. It's better to find someone else to run the clipper through your hair, probably changing up the guard for the top and bottom of your noggin. The cut that's served me well for more than a decade is a No. 6 up high and a No. 1 down low. In order to steer clear of mushroom head, have your haircutting slave bridge the line between the two layers by running the clippers over a comb pressed against your noggin. For those with longer hair, I hear good things about the Flowbee. Okay, not really, but it's got to work better than a bowl cut.

Oh to be alive in the 1970s, when long hair was deemed a fashionable quality. Those hippies from back in the day could get away without a haircut for months, and when they really needed one, they could hack it off themselves with scissors. In return for this luxury, they had to live with polyester pants and chest-hair-exposing leisure suits.

It makes me proud to cruise the streets and still catch glimpses of those brave, bold souls who rock hippie hair in modern times. It takes a true hippie soul to let his long, wavy hair speak for him and subvert the powers that be—fashion faux pas consequences be damned.

5. Don't Smoke

Not much mystery to this advice: Listen to Nancy and just say no. Never try a cigarette, even if you're thirteen and all the cool kids are doing it, because you'll be set down the path of ending up a yellow-toothed, chimney-breathed, black-lunged cancer tub. And you'll be poor. The government has tacked so many taxes onto these suckers that it's cheaper to fund an endless war in the Middle East than it is to fulfill your cig habit for ten years. Look it up.

I may have been exaggerating there, but the average annual cost of sustaining a cigarette habit is actually $1,500, which doesn't even count your higher healthcare premiums or clothes and furniture you ruin with cigarette burns.

The funny thing is that smokers, in general, are the cheapest bastards you'll ever find. They're always asking one another for cigarettes, and the ones that have them always lie and say they don't have any, which is okay because the people who are asking actually have some of their own but don't want to dip into their own supplies. Sometimes I even ask people for cigarettes, just so I can break them in front of their faces, demonstrating what an awful habit it is. Fine, I'll admit I've never actually done that, but my drunken friend did so one night to a waitress at the Waffle House, and I was so impressed I've adopted his story as my own.

If only those of us who aren't drunken lunatics would take such active measures. Instead, too many of us are just whiny, preaching dipshits whose complaints fall on deaf ears. The

worst offenders are passive-aggressive wimps who cast a scowl at anyone who lights up. Smokers thrive on such reactions—most even ask permission before they smoke, knowing full well they won't be denied—and they know you won't actually be so bold as to say something to them, even if they blow the putrid fumes right into your face. Dirty looks only act as encouragement.

Some nonsmokers complain that smokers drive up the cost of health coverage because of their higher sickness rate, but that's really a lie because health insurers are out to screw you however possible and will always charge the highest rates they can regardless of the health habits of those they cover. Smoking is decreasing in popularity, yet healthcare premiums continue to magically rise.

Nonsmokers always tell smokers that they're killing themselves, but the addicts just laugh it off. They don't believe it because all their friends smoke and they're all doing just fine. The tragedy isn't that cigarettes cause lung cancer; it's that they don't cause it fast enough. This isn't a wish, mind you, that all smokers would die, but just that they could see some tangible effects from their habit and have more of an impetus to fight it off. Because smoking just doesn't pay.

Eating

They say you are what you eat. I say you are what you save on eating. It should go without saying that the worst thing you can do, if you're trying to save money on food, is to be bulimic. If you must have an eating disorder, go with anorexia. It's the bargain of the compulsory, self-starving, dining neuroses.

6. Double Your Pleasure, Double Your Fries

Fast-food french fries are oh so tasty, but how, you may ask, might you double your order without doubling the price? The answer is to get a little help from your pal the ice cube. Just gobble down half your fries, then gather your chilly, cubic friend in the palm of your hand and toss him into the container. Presto! Soggy fries. Dump the spoiled remainder onto your tray, so as to hide the amount of how many you've already eaten, then march the mess back up to the counter and demand a replacement batch posthaste. You'll be rewarded with a fresh set of artery-clogging delights, and most of the time you'll even get to keep the soggy fries that are splayed on your tray. And admit it, you'll be happy about that, because you have low standards and don't really mind whether your fries are wet, stale, limp, or burned.

Be careful, however, not to allow your enthusiasm to get the best of you, tempting you to hurry along too quickly. Once, while attempting this ruse on a drive-through trip while listening to the American League Championship series on the radio, I plopped my cube into a gaggle of steaming fries, positive the heat would melt the ice by the time I could circle back through the line. Without even checking, I handed the fry cup through the window, only to be left hanging for several seconds of uncertainty. I wondered what the problem was—did I oversell my anger? Did I pantomime my lie by staring off into space as I pleaded my case? The manager emerged from the window with a damning glare in his eyes.

"There's an ice cube in here," he said, handing me the un-doubled fries.

"Oh, right," I said with a gulp, grabbing the food while avoiding eye contact, and then speeding off in shame.

Of course, it's a given that if you frequent a place that routinely hands out soggy fries, you won't have to go through the described charade. In fact, I've found that nearly 90 percent of fast-food items are immediately returnable due to some sort of flaw, thanks to how little effort or craftsmanship goes into their making. I wish I could take credit for the idea, but in all honesty it comes from the "Where's the beef?" lady. She was a genius far ahead of her time.

7. Your Backseat Artillery

In the Old West, desperados would never go any-where without their six-shooters. Nowadays wanton arms toting is somewhat frowned upon, but you can carry the idea into other aspects of life. My favorite application is the free fast-food drink refill—more on that in a minute.

Glory be to those out-in-the-open soda foun-tains, bastions of the thirsty home-less man, who will calmly enter any fast-food joint as if it was his mom's house and fill his thermos with Mr. Pibb as the pimple-faced teen behind the cash register pre-tends not to notice.

When the drinks are unguarded, there's no stopping you from loading up unabated. Things get a bit trickier, however, when the soda fountain is located behind the cash register.

While we can all dream of a bright future in which the archaic practice of well-defended sodas has been eliminated, we must protect our-selves with a six-shooter equivalent for the twenty-first century. I suggest you establish a cup-collection spree on your usual dining rounds and not stop until you've set yourself up with at least six cups that allow you access to the spectrum of whatever food you might come to be in the mood for. A well-rounded portfolio might include Subway, Wendy's, Carl's Jr., McDonald's, Burger King, and Taco Bell. Rinse them out after each use and store them in the backseat of your car.

Are you following me here? Should you ever become parched as you're making your travels and happen upon one of the restaurants emblazoned with a logo that matches one of the cups in your arsenal, pull it out and storm through the double doors. Hand the cup to the cashier and explain how you'd like a refill. You might get a weird look, but you'll get what you ask for.

In my experience, I've found that cups tend to endure eight to ten refills before becoming too weak and tattered to continue worthwhile service. Every now and then, however, I'm surprised by how long those cardboard suckers can last. I've got a Wendy's cup sitting in my car that I'm pretty sure hasn't been replaced since 2003. Maybe Wendy's uses stronger cardboard than the other chains. Maybe I haven't gone to Wendy's as much as I have its burger rivals. Or maybe, just maybe, all the bacteria that have grown inside the cup have reinforced its walls. No matter—I don't question the process, I just appreciate the results.

8. Happy Birthday to Me

I've never understood why it is that people make a big deal about birthdays. Sure, they're fun when you're six, but every birthday after sixteen feels like another nail in the coffin. Maybe all the festivities are there to counteract the depression that comes with having your age jacked yet another notch higher.

At least there's one facet of the birthday blues to get excited about—the obligatory restaurant birthday cake. Most restaurants partake in the tradition, although many will force you to suffer through an embarrassing group serenade from the waitstaff before allowing you to partake. Even if you're not sure that the restaurant at which you're eating is down with this sickness, it's a good idea to always tell the waiter it's your birthday. It'll work unless you're ordering drinks and are carded. Sometimes you'll get the cake, sometimes you'll get an appetizer or discount, sometimes you'll get nothing—which is what you'd get anyway if you neglect to lie and say it's your birthday. I'd be about 4,750 years old if I were telling the truth every time I announced it was my birthday during a meal out.

The lower-end, family-type places, such as Denny's, even give out free meals, but there's no telling how long the foolish practice will hold up given the poor economy. Several restaurants still give out free birthday grubs to kids under age ten, but unless you happen to be nine or under with a birthday coming up, that won't do you much good.

At Sweet Tomatoes they have this promotion called Club Veg, which spams you with the restaurant's specials throughout the year but rewards you by e-mailing you a buy one, get one free coupon a couple weeks before your birthday. The beauty of e-coupons, especially those with no serial code imprinted on the certificates, is that they can be printed out again and again. The Club Veg coupons don't expire until two weeks after your birthday; so needless to say, you and a friend have got a month of half-priced meals coming your way. Get a partner in on it, and that's nearly a sixth of the year you've got covered in Club Veg bliss. And if you're a little creative in signing up for the promotion under a few different e-mail addresses, you can celebrate your "birthday" with cheap soup and salad on a perpetual basis.

Corporate policies change so often—usually for the worse—that it's not worth posting a comprehensive list here, but work the phones and "the Google" and you'll be surprised at the various perks faux birthdays can yield. Free movies, mugs, rentals, and even oil changes can be had if you keep your greedy little feelers on alert.

9. I'll Save on This Purchase, Thankyouverymuch

O ften in your travels up and down the supermarket aisles you'll run into specially marked packages of something or other, with stuck-on coupons good for your next purchase. You have my permission to go ahead and discreetly remove those coupons right then and there, and use them on this purchase (or save for when the item is marked down on a sale). In fact, why not play it to the bone and strip each coupon off every package in stock just because it's so easy to do? Even useless coupons for products you'd never buy are worth something, although the figure is usually far less than the value of the paper on which it's printed.

Pay close attention to the fine print on coupons and you'll note that each one carries a cash value of $\frac{1}{100}$ of a cent. That means, and I just looked it up online to prove it, that for every 100 coupons you collect, you're due a shiny penny from the issuing company in return. Every 10,000 coupons you can muster together are worth a dollar, and every 10 billion coupons are worth a million bucks. It's my fantasy to one day collect ten billion of the same type of coupon and use them to become a millionaire. It could happen if I got everyone in China to collect ten coupons for me. I'm so gonna do it.

10. Dining Like a Cheap SOB

Some look upon eating as one of life's great pleasures, but I see it as a miserable inconvenience—a tedious ritual that drains your funds and sidetracks you from productive activities. Hours of elaborate preparation can go into just one meal, and if you're not careful you can find yourself falling into a cycle in which all you're doing is either eating or preparing to eat. And as much of a hassle as food is coming into our bodies, it's even more annoying coming out. What percentage of our lives, I wonder, is spent on toilets? Oh, to be a cyborg with a rechargeable battery. That must be why Walt Disney and Ted Williams had themselves frozen, in hopes of awakening to a marvelous electronic utopia in which turkey and mashed potatoes can be downloaded into their digital brains. Yum . . .

But alas, in the twenty-first century our bodies are still addicted to food and its distractions, but luckily I'm here to help you minimize its burden.

With years of practice I've managed to hone my cheap son-of-a-bitch dining skills to a razor-sharp level. Nearly every ounce of food I consume is done so in the quickest and lowest-possible-cost manner, and now I will share my knowledge. Live by these tenets and you can be exactly as awesome as I.

First, don't ever cook—I can't believe there's an entire TV network devoted to the tiresome process of making food. I've seen these shows in which people grin into the camera and share moronic banter with their cohosts as they pour mixed dump-gloop into pans and puff out their chests pridefully once it's all cooked and ready to go. I feel bad for these people, actually—have they never heard of Hungry Man? Once, in the interest of anthropological study, I sat through a thirty-minute show about two jackasses making Salisbury steak. Do they realize that thanks to Hungry Man I can make fifteen of these in the time it takes them to make one? And mine will even taste better, thanks to the wondrous preservatives and tasty chemicals mixed into my imitation meat.

Thanks to processed, prepackaged foods that can be heated quickly, there is no longer a need for cookbooks, ingredients, or even utensils and tables. These frozen delights are best consumed with your bare hands while leaning over the kitchen counter or garbage can. I could easily eat frozen pizzas for every meal the rest of my life without complaint. My favorite defrost-able dinners are store-brand thin pizzas, which can be had for $2 or less, and the aforementioned Hungry Man meals, which usually range from $2 to $4. For lunch I go for the Banquet Pepperoni Pizza Meal (88 cents at my Wal-Mart and comes with pudding) and mix in corn dogs, which are more cost-effective than their cousins, hot dogs, due to the lack of the perishable bun co-component. Ever try matching the amount of hot dogs you buy to a package of buns? You have to buy three eight-packs of dogs and four bun six-packs to make it work, and since the buns are rarely sold with expiration dates longer than two weeks out, odds are you'll be throwing half of them away. So not worth it.

A second piece of key advice is to only drink water. It's free, it won't rot your teeth, and it goes with everything. Drinking soda or booze with every meal is a good way to drive yourself into the poorhouse, whereas avoiding those vices will make you rich beyond your wildest dreams. I once read that Bill Gates became a billionaire not by inventing Microsoft but by giving up Mr. Pibb. *Fine*, I only read that because I wrote it, but you get the idea.

The one exception to the water rule applies when you're at a fast-food joint with an unguarded soda fountain that stupidly gives you the water cup you ask for, then blindly allows you to fill it up with Mountain Dew instead.

While we're on the subject of fast-food joints, never fall for the ruse of the value meal menus, which up sell you into ridiculously large drinks you don't need to be paying for. Always order your food à la carte, preferably off the "99 cent" menu. And if your place of choice has no such menu, stop patronizing it until it does. Arby's is sure to come around one day thanks to the pressure applied by my personal embargo. Wendy's thought it would pull a smart-ass move by raising the cost of their double stacks from 99 cents to $1.39 (or thereabouts), but guess what happened? I stopped buying them and now their business is probably ruined. No way am I about to let one chain unilaterally up my burger budget by 40 percent. We, as a consumer society, need to hold strong on this 99-cent threshold.

You may wonder why I've thus far skipped breakfast, and my answer is that I recommend you do exactly that—don't fall for the dairy and cereal-propagated myth that breakfast is the most important meal of the day. It's an unnecessary custom that should be avoided if at all possible, although if you've become too addicted to the rite over the years, I suggest loading up on bulk frozen waffles, flavored with syrup packets you pocketed from a burger joint. Milk and cereal, which I admit I've fallen victim to consuming on a regular basis, are problematic because milk has a short fridge-life. Oddly enough, the combo is still cost-effective if you use it for dinners.

11. There *is* Such a Thing as a Free Lunch

Whoever said there's no such thing as a free lunch has never frequented the grocery store sample booth circuit, especially at warehouse wholesale stores such as Costco or Sam's Club, which boast the most bountiful setups. In forty-five minutes of sample stalking, you can round up a feast worthy of royalty.

On many a weekend day I avoid eating lunch in favor of vulturing my way up and down the aisles, swooping in to scavenge bits of free food from trays guarded by senile, old codgers until I've had my fill. I used to be stealthy and crafty in the way I went about my sampling, grabbing a bagel bit here, hitting the next aisle over for a cup of trail mix before cycling backward for a shot of punch, then sneaking a second bagel bit. This was when I still tried to maintain a semblance of dignity. But no more. Now I'll shamelessly scoop up entire handfuls of whatever I can, stuffing all that will fit into my mouth and the rest into my pockets. I'm happy to report that you can do so with impunity. The minimum-wage slaves who shell out the free eats couldn't care less who gets the food, only that they get rid of it all as quickly as possible. And those workers who do get annoyed when I swipe half a tray's worth of the Hormel chili they've spent fifteen minutes setting up almost never say anything when I make my heist because they're too stunned at my move. And I silence those who do open their yaps by claiming I'm getting some extras for friends or family.

The sample cart lunch hour is no secret, so you've got to be bold and decisive as you make your rounds. Imagine one of those documentaries about the lion on the prowl, times it by twelve, and that's the sort of competition you're in for. Lines tend to congregate around the stands set up for the more popular items, but feel free to ignore them and just rush in to do what you must. Personally, I prefer avoiding real competition and preying on the weak. I'll box out a gaggle of great-grandmas in order to snare a salmon-on-rye square-let. I'll dart in front of a five-year-old to take the last slice of ice cream bar. Hey, the kid has to learn sometime that slowness is never rewarded. Only when a man who's clearly bigger and tougher than I gets to a sample cart before I do will I impatiently wait in line for my turn. Luckily, few sample scavengers are bodybuilders.

Two schools of thought differ on whether to strike up a verbal interplay with your food donors or to take what's yours without so much as eye contact. I can see benefits to both. It's worth getting to know the kindly welfare granny who's in charge of the DiGiorno half-slices. A little feigned interest in her bingo night and maybe some coy flirtation here and there and she'll not only fill you in on when the next batch will be ready for you, she may even slip you a whole piece with

FREE SAMPLES

a wink. On the other hand, there's a hefty benefit in avoiding conversation in order to save time, as well as not allow feelings to jeopardize your maneuvers. Say you approach the DiGiorno granny, while out of the corner of your eye you see Caramel Apple Guy is setting up his wares. Due to your courtesy in chatting up your pizza-picking pal, you may be a step slow in beating out the snot-nosed brats for dessert. Choose your path wisely and be willing to live with your decisions.

12. Potluck Grinch

Invitations to potlucks used to annoy me, before I saw the events for what they are—advantageous opportunities to capitalize on the culinary work of others while providing almost nothing in return. Such meals are exercises in grandiose competition between cooks willing to prove their worth by dazzling one another with their tasty creations. Those who benefit from all the one-upmanship are the ones who have the least to bring to the table, like me.

Most of the time, potlucks occur at work, often late in the year when your department's catering budget for monthly meetings has dwindled to nil and the boss posts a sign-up sheet. The wisest play is, of course, to avoid this sheet altogether, perhaps stepping out or taking an imaginary phone call at your desk when the party ringleader makes the call out for volunteers. Establishing a Reaganesque plausible deniability that you knew a potluck was taking place at all makes it much easier for you to plead your case the day of the party, and thus be allowed to join the buffet line with all the contributors.

If the list-call is unavoidable, perhaps sent out in a staff e-mail or sadistically announced to each person individually, your best bet is to declare you have a meeting or doctor's appointment that conflicts with the date. Then you can cancel your imaginary responsibility just before the potluck and glumly show up without a lunch. Odds are you'll still be invited to join in the face-stuffing.

You can only skip out altogether on so many potluck sign-ups without drawing a reputation, so a smarter alternative is to sign up for something menial, such as chips or rolls, then "forget" to bring them when judgment day arrives. Most of the time no one will notice that you didn't ante up. An alternate track involves signing up for something generic someone has already volunteered to bring, such as ice, chips, or soda. Because your category will be covered by the guy who signed up first, you'll be off the hook when you "forget" your fare.

If you've exhausted other options and absolutely must bring something to the potluck, make it utensils or napkins. You can bring stuff you've got at home, or grab it for free at a fast-food place on your way into the office. If you're one of those hoity-toity types who has something against handing out napkins with the telltale Pizza Hut logo stamped on them, a visit to a dollar store will serve your needs with minimum financial damage.

If absolutely all else fails, and you must buy some sort of food to bring along, buy the most disgusting, bizarre snack you can think of—maybe chili-flavored chocolate cookies from the Mexican aisle—then stick the unopened package near the back of the table. If everything goes right, no one will touch your revolting contribution and you'll be able to return it to the place of purchase the next day for a full refund.

13. Tupperware Thief

Leftovers should make up the base of the pyramid of any cheapskate's diet. But the base will spoil too quickly for maximum consumption unless it's encased in airtight plastic.

Tupperware and its derivatives are a key component of your cupboard. Marvels of modern science, these containers work exactly like the green-spotted, one-up mushrooms in "Super Mario Bros."—providing extra lives to your unfinished pizza, tacos, and breakfast burritos. And like one-up Mario 'shrooms, which run 100 golden coins, the devices are relatively pricey. Well, they're actually not all that expensive, but as Johnny Appleseed taught us all, you should never, ever pay for something that grows on trees. Tupperware fruit happens to spring from the branches of your family tree.

Whenever there's a giant, food-involved get-together—family gatherings are your best bet, but any social occasion will work—the host always unloads leftovers to all takers. Many partygoers demurely deny the free food, often either because they're stuffed or because all the good grub has been picked over and only the rancid slop is left. Instead of conjuring a polite way to tell Aunt Becky you're not into her warmed-over yams, offer gladly to accept not only those but her rutabaga surprise casserole that not even the flies dared to touch. She'll be so grateful you're willing to tolerate her repulsive bile that she won't even think to ask that you return the accompanying packaging. Because you're a kindhearted gentleman, you'll wait until you're out of the neighborhood before you toss the food out the car window on the drive back home, rubbing your hands in exuberant accomplishment that you've just scored semipermanent housing for the Swedish meatballs you've currently got wrapped in reused tinfoil.

Sometimes the Tupperware donor will send you off with a winking, passive-aggressive parting shot, such as, "Oh, don't worry about bringing back that container soon—I'll hunt you down for it if need be." People can get mighty territorial about their food storage stuffs. Feel free to affably retort, "I definitely plan on stealing it and keeping it forever. You won't get it back without a fight!" Which is hilariously true. If they ever do ask for it back, insist you returned it a long time ago, right after you were done using it. When they question the veracity of your claim, snap back, "Oh, I'm so sorry you're hard up for Tupperware these days. Would you like to come over to my house and take some of mine? I have too much, really. You'd be doing me a favor."

This will stop them cold every time, because it not only belittles them by making them feel petty for caring so much about something so insignificant, it casts a pall of inferiority on them by hinting you've got more Tupperware than they do. Comparing the sizes of your Tupperware collections is a lot like measuring pissing streams.

14. Kids Eat Free

My favorite Dwight Shrute moment in the TV show *The Office* comes in a Season Three episode in which the straight-talking, bespectacled nerf-herder asks a guy at a party whether or not he watches *Battlestar Galactica*. When he responds "no," Dwight shoots back, "Then you are an idiot."

Such is my sentiment to parents who only take their kids out to eat at restaurants during the weekends, and thus miss out on all the weekday kids-eat-free promotions that take place at seemingly every family dining establishment.

Just as Dwight's dogged banter convinced me to rent the DVDs of the TV show—by the way, he's right, so rent the DVDs like right now—I hope you emerge from this chapter determined to no longer follow the socially-conditioned routine of eating out on the weekends and in on the weekdays. This is a financially counterintuitive practice, since the costs rise on busy weekend nights and dip during the traditionally slower-paced off-days. This is especially true for families, whose dining-out costs rise exponentially depending on size. If you're saddled with rugrats, you'll do best to pack it in on the weekends and step out Monday through Thursday, when you'll always find better specials and the cur-aziest promotions; the craziest of these being the kids-eat-free hook. Web sites such as Kidseatfree.com will clue you in to deals in your specific locale, but places that offer this gig usually aren't too shy about it. They're desperate to do anything to fill their empty chairs during slow nights.

A big family can descend on a place that offers this and run it out of business. I have only two children, but seeing these deals makes me want to go all Catholic/Mormon and crank out a dozen whippersnappers just so I can exact a maximum killing level. The deal usually forces your youngsters to order off a special kids' menu, with one-third the portions, but what do your kids care? They aren't gonna eat it anyway. They'll just run around the table like maniacs and throw rolls at one another like they always do. At least you won't have to subsidize the madness.

Savvy restaurants include fine print that requires each free kids' dish to be accompanied by a full-priced adult entrée purchase. This can be subverted by a cranky rant at the manager once the check comes. You can claim you were tricked and plan on complaining to the Better Business Bureau unless he makes good on what you thought the promotion was. If you're denied, you should always loudly complain to the dining room that you were gypped and you'll never eat at this restaurant again. You'll either be thrown out or kowtowed to.

15. Price Mash

Nearly every supermarket nowadays runs a price-matching program meant to satisfy customers' nagging suspicion that they're charging more than the competition for a lot of their stuff. The policy is present more as a security blanket than anything else, set in place by corporate bigwigs who figure not enough customers will actually go through the labor-intensive process to save a few cents off their pinto beans and slash into their stores' profit margins.

This way of thinking makes a lot of sense. To make sure you're saving the maximum amount, you need to jot down an ironclad shopping list, obsessively scan every newspaper ad, and then set up a spreadsheet that helps you annotate the ads with the pertinent low prices at each store. Do all that, and you're rewarded with the opportunity to make everyone standing in line behind you want to shoot you in the back of the head because you're holding things up by making the cashier verify each price.

But there is another way—a way that skips several of the steps and saves you more money than even the most anal-retentive, price-match maven.

Here's what you'll need: a stack of sticky notes, a pen, and an armful of glossy grocery store ads. Lug all that into the shopping cart and you're in business. Affix one of your Post-its to every non-store-brand item you come across, then name your own price, making sure to deduct a substantial but not-quite-insane amount from the price tag. You use the pen to jot down the "price-matched" figure you're willing to pay for each item, and you can even go the extra mile for feigned authenticity by adding in a random competing store name to each sticky note.

As you approach the front of the checkout line, the checkout lady will immediately attempt to head out on break. But she'll warm to you once she sees how organized you are, and will happily tap your savings into the register. In most cases, the checkout clerk will be so confounded with the hassle she'll approve all your prices just to keep the line moving.

Only the most bored or crazy checkout folk will sort through that unwieldy stack of ads to verify your sales notations are accurate, or compare your prices with their online database of competitors' sales, but it's still wise to avoid shopping during off-hours in order to avoid empty lines. The busier the store is, the better.

Relationships

No facet of your existence will drain your net worth more than your love life, unless you happen to be one of the many women who have married Donald Trump or one of the many men who have married Britney Spears. Remember to steer away from prostitutes, who, despite what their pimps may argue, are never good investments.

16. Yay WNBA

As you flip through the newspaper sports section or watch SportsCenter, it's common to wonder, "Why the hell does the WNBA exist?" The answer is twofold. One is to provide a

role model for young girls, teaching them that basketball isn't as pointless as softball or soccer and could actually pay off if they work hard enough. Never mind that most players make less than your garbageman. The other reason is to provide silver-bullet dates for horny young men looking to pretend they're evolved and sophisticated.

It's the second purpose of existence we'll focus on here.

While the average real NBA ticket price is about $50, the average WNBA admission is less than $15, meaning you won't have to sell your spleen on the black market in order to afford a game, parking, and a soda.

Volunteering to go to women's athletic events elevates you to heroic status in the eyes of your potential beloved. All their lives, athletic-minded ladies have had their endeavors belittled and marginalized by even the men they love the most, but you emerge as a white knight who appears to actually take an interest in girls' meaningless sporting pursuits. You can boost your credibility by reading up on the teams involved so you can toss off little inside-baseball-ish tidbits as you watch the game unfold. And because the tickets cost so little, you won't even need to wince when she orders at the concession stand.

The irony is women's athletics are pretty interesting to watch. In my years as a sportswriter I came to appreciate the earnest, unsullied competition offered by women's sports. The fundamentals are sound, and there's no me-first showboating that plagues men's games. And it also doesn't hurt that each team has a player that's pretty damn hot.

While it's true there are cheaper sporting events to attend, say, high school games, there's no way you can go to one of those without appearing creepy. Either you take her to a boys basketball game and look like a loser who's trying to relive his scant former athletic glory, or you go to a girls game and look like a kid-ogling freakazoid. College athletic events, though, are doable, especially if you live out of range of pro organizations. Should you be dating a girl who's into volleyball, you can do no better for the both of you than by taking her to a college volleyball match. No sport, save for gymnastics and figure skating, which are exhibitions rather than competitions, has its competitors wear sluttier outfits. Volleyball girls wear spandex shorts with knee pads (!), tight T-shirts with their sleeves tucked under, and they're trained to wait for the ball while bending over. I swear this game must have been invented by Russ Meyer. Volleyball earns even more points because it takes place indoors, meaning you won't be drenched in sweat the way you would be at a soccer or softball game, and admission, unlike basketball, is usually free.

17. The Dutch Are a Wise and Just People

Now that we're well into the new millennium, let's give a nod to feminism and forever cast aside the antiquated notion that guys should pay for everything on dates. Failing that, let's at least get both genders to agree that whoever pays for dinner is guaranteed sex afterward. No more of this insinuation, mixed signals, and implied assumption garbage. Relationships are complicated enough without further convoluting things with money. It would be so much easier if there were a hidebound rule that a Dutch date determines equality, while a paid date means prostitution. Fair, yes?

It's true that I only dare say this because I'm married and thus never expect to go out on another date in my life. But why women should be offended at this notion is beyond comprehension. Even though I'm the stingiest, most rotten-hearted shyster I've ever known or heard of, I can't imagine allowing a woman whom I didn't want to have sex with pay for our evening out together. I'd feel cruel and immoral, and believe me, for me to feel that way about anything it has to be pretty darn intense. So strongly do I hold this belief that imagining some nasty leviathan paying for my meal makes me not only squeamish but also angry.

I picture myself out with Rosie O'Donnell, who for the purposes of this antifantasy fashions me as the one dude who's so irresistible she'd drop her life partner for. I agree if only for the novelty and the conversation, and I cringe on my side of the table as she eats the ogre's share of our giant platter of nachos. When the waiter comes and offers the check, she seizes it and refuses to let me toss in my share. At this point I'd be so livid—having determined that she's thinking she's going to make sweet love to me afterward—I'd wrench the sucker out of her Twinkie-plumped hands with unbridled fury.

Ahem. As I was saying, there's nothing wrong with splitting things down the middle or, in order to avoid the awkwardness of calculations, change-swapping and check-cutting—working out a system in which one person pays at one outing while the other picks up the check next time out. This should be done without conversation or analysis, and the onus falls just as much on the guy to allow the lady to pay as it does on the lady to seriously offer.

And lest some of you imagine that it's a foolhardy notion to imagine a situation in which a sugar-momma takes over and offers to cover your finances, I direct you to the tale of my friend we'll call "Roy." He once dated a woman who paid his share of the rent—while he was my roommate—bought him groceries, and even did his laundry. Roy would share stories of his unorthodox situation with me in a combination of giddiness and unease. I told him that he'd repay all the money she spent on him with his life if he ever dared to break up with her, and the entire time I lived with him I feared she'd catch Roy on one of the many times he cheated on her and burn our apartment to the ground. Thankfully that never happened. She just got sick of him and broke it off herself. I guess she found Roy to be no longer worth the monthly payments.

18. Art of the Well-timed Fight/Breakup

Always keep a mental list of everything that angers you about your significant other. You'll need it as ammunition for when you need to start spontaneous fights at key junctures.

While it may seem counterintuitive to ever intentionally start an argument, especially if you're with the type who likes to hit, throw things, or scream, learning and practicing the art of the well-timed fight or break-up can save you untold thousands of dollars over your relationship.

I recommend at least four, I-never-wanna-see-you-again (till next week) throw-downs: Valentine's Day, her birthday, your anniversary, and Christmas. Throw Thanksgiving in there too if her parents annoy you and she's asked you to dine with her family.

The goal here is to avoid buying presents. Picture two people: Man A and Man B. Man A is a common, stout-hearted chap who sticks with the woman he loves through thick and thin, dutifully buying her flowers ($50) for V-Day, a necklace ($100) for her birthday, springing for a fancy dinner ($90) to

celebrate their anniversary, and buying her a camera ($300) for Christmas. Meanwhile Man B tells his girl she looks fat in that dress on February 12, exclaims he doesn't like her cooking the week before her birthday, asks her if she's ever considered getting a boob job just before their anniversary, and declares he never wants to get married on December 23. Add it up and you'll discover Man B has saved more than $500 by behaving like a douche. And the epilogue to this little hypothetical is that Man A is dumped by his girlfriend in early January because she felt guilty that she got drunk and made out with Man B at a New Year's party. Why? Because nice guys finish last and women love assholes.

I know some people who rigorously start fights before each of these dreaded, recurring, gift-soaking occurrences. My pal Mike takes it to a further extreme, dropping whoever he's with altogether when the dates roll around. He boasts that he has never stayed with the same girl for more than six months. While Mike has foolishly sacrificed make-up sex, there's plenty of validity to his actions. As for myself, I'm sad to report that the money-saving power of the art of the well-timed fight no longer works once you're well into the fourth year of marriage.

Household

Remember when you were a teenager and started acting up? Poppa told you, "Under my roof, you'll live by my rules." Well, now that you no longer live with your dad, he no longer has authority over how you run your household. But guess what? You're still taking orders from your parents and your spouse. And since you're reading this book, you're also taking orders from me. So do what I say or you'll regret it. And put the cap back on the toothpaste or I'll take away your allowance.

19. Things You Never Ever Have to Buy

Every time I'm in a supermarket line and I see someone buying a stack of napkins, a jar of mustard, or a tube of ketchup, I cry. Well, actually I just shake my head and thank all that's holy that I'm not as dumb as the person buying those things. If you part with money in exchange for things that come for free, you may as well pay for water or radio. Oh, wait.

Just as it makes no sense to buy Evian or get a satellite radio subscription, it's nonsensical to buy things attainable in perfectly good, mini plastic squeeze-packs at fast-food joints.

Whenever I stop in to grab a value meal, I'm sure to get the maximum value by cramming my pockets with whatever condiments packets I come across. The practice is so second nature for me that it's now really first nature. I think of stocking up on mustard—oh, that tangy nectar that doubles the goodness of hot dogs—before I even remember that I came there to eat. In my home I keep a giant bucket filled with enough salsa, relish, and Arby's sauce to last a family of seven well into the twenty-second century.

Personally I'm fine with tearing open each packet individually, but that may not be everyone's speed. A slick alternative is to get all your ripping and squeezing out of the way off the bat, draining your collective harvest into a single jar. Whatever you need to do to make yourself happy.

Syrup, butter, honey, ranch dressing—all these can be had ad infinitum if you make your rounds through any reputable food court or strip mall. The toughest part is building up your stash when you're just getting started. A backpack is highly recommended.

The bounty you can reap from fast-food places stretches far beyond simple sauces, however. Be sure to take maximum advantage of straw and especially napkin dispensers. The latter will make it so you'll never need paper towels, coasters, or dishcloths. The potential usage of napkins is nearly infinite—collect enough and you can use them to line your hamster cage, spot-shine your windows, or even dry yourself in lieu of bath towels. I strongly advise against pushing your fast-food napkins to the natural extension of toilet-side, butt-wiping companion. Those suckers clog up toilets like nobody's business, and, yes, I know this from experience. When I was nineteen, my roommates and I flooded our apartment because we foolishly used napkins as toilet paper for several months. When the janitor came to fix the toilet he asked us if we were using napkins as toilet paper, and we of course denied it.

"Yeah, you are," he said confidently. "Don't do that anymore."

We nodded in sheepish concurrence.

20. Wipe It Clean

When you're driving down the freeway and fate sends a rock careening toward your visage, it's a natural reaction to curse, yell, or even try to veer your car to avoid the collision. And yet all are incorrect. Whenever your windshield gets cracked, you're actually entering a stroke of luck.

Such is the competition among glass companies that they'll sink to incredible depths to earn your business. Free meals, hundreds of dollars off your deductible, and even cash are all possibilities. I imagine what's going on here is these businesses are competing to exploit insurance companies, charging them such ridiculous sums for windshield replacements that they're willing to pay you just for the honor of working on your car.

Obviously you can't take advantage of this situation unless you've got glass coverage. While I'm theoretically against nearly all insurance that's not mandated by law, I back down when it comes to glass. In my experience it adds no more than a few bucks to your monthly premium—often nothing at all—and you can always easily make up the difference by seeking out the companies offering the best deals.

Your insurance agency usually harbors a relationship with a "recommended glass shop," and for this reason it's best to call the company you'd like to use directly. They'll take care of the three-way call to your insurance agent, who will back down and approve the claim unless he has some sort of personal vendetta against the company you'd like to use. Go the alternate route and your agent will shepherd you to their Scrooge-like partner who won't give you any extras.

I've found that many of the most lucrative deals come from fixers who literally run the business out of the backs of their trucks. These guys have low overhead and not only give up the most to get your attention; they'll even come to your house and workplace to do the job. I've collected $50–$60 checks on several occasions from such entrepreneurs. My experiences with those companies that advertise twenty-four free meals on TV have been less positive. Those food coupons often are stuck with restrictions that allow them only to be used on weekdays or are only buy-one, get-one-free. Always talk out the particulars of the bonus deals with the guy on the phone before you give him your insurance agent's phone number.

21. These Crazy Kids

There are two ways you can look at the privileged upper class. Either curse them with scorn and whine about how the system is made so the fat cats get to stay on top while exploiting the labors of the working stiffs like you; or, just happily accept the way things are and try to mooch off whatever the blue bloods' children throw away into dorm Dumpsters at the end of the school year.

As you might gather, I adhere to the latter. You'd be amazed—amazed! I tell you—at the quality of treasures these spoiled, trust-fund babies discard. Not only do garbage receptacles in late May overflow with the standard dorm fare, such as midget refrigerators, beanbags, hot plates, and posters, but they also pack cooler stuff than a Best Buy clearance sale. I'm talking microwaves, CD players, speakers, computers, stereos, and TVs. Pampered students ditch most of the items because they can't be bothered to lug them back to their parents' homes for the summer, and the thought of heading to a pawnshop is unthinkable. These are kids with enough money on mommy's and daddy's credit cards to replace everything they get rid of without a thought.

Collecting these riches is not without its risks. Whenever you're Dumpster diving, you're going to have to compete with homeless people. And not the beaten-down, lazy homeless you find sprawled on street corners—I'm talking the aggressive go-getters who need to scavenge for items in order to support their chemical addictions. I'd advise steering clear of direct confrontations with street folk who have gotten to your quarry before you arrive, lest you want to risk getting a rum bottle shiv stuck in your back while you're wiping spaghetti sauce off a Toshiba monitor. The easy way to dispatch your competitors is with a quick phone call to campus police. A bike-peddling U-cop has nothing better to do than hassle the homeless, brushing them off with nightsticks and inadvertently clearing the way for taxpayers such as yourself. Just be sure to give the officers enough time to scamper off to their next assignment before starting your gold rush, since they'll likely chase you away as well.

Because the phenomenon of wasteful dorm dwellers is so well known—there are actually stories about this in the newspapers—you need to be especially focused on getting to the trash bin as soon as the goods become available. This requires

keeping an eye on a few key dates on the online campus calendar: the final day of classes, the last day of finals, and the day resident houses close. All three occasions will supply a heavy flow of trinkets all for your taking.

A final word of warning: Keep an eye to the sky. Students commonly use windows positioned directly above the Dumpster to give their departing items easy send-offs. The careless kids will toss their DVD players without first scanning below for an all-clear, and some of the meaner kids—the future CEOs and HR managers—will even aim at you. Remember, the object is to take useless things from the trash bin, not to become a useless object yourself whose corpse is permanently stuck on a dorm sidewalk.

22. Paydirt

The phrase "cheaper than dirt" is a misnomer. Whenever you need to haul a metric ton or so into your backyard for a landscaping project, you can expect to pay $20 or more. Tack on another $40 for delivery and $100 to carry and spread it in your yard. That's a pretty pricey proposition for something that's lying around everywhere for free. Bear in mind, I'm talking regular old dirt here, not gold dust, fine-grain sand, or nutrition-enriched soil.

And yet, if you buy a house—which you definitely should do to avoid the rent trap—you may well find yourself paying for dirt, all the while moaning about how awful and unfair it is. You'd be surprised how often you need huge piles of dirt to do nearly anything creative with your yard. If you want a raised-bed garden with a retaining wall, you'll need to fill it with dirt. If you're filling a dilapidated pool, you'll need a bunch of dirt. Planting a tree? Lotsa dirt. Putting in an irrigation system? Dirt. And if you take it from your own backyard, you'll just end up with a giant, unsightly hole.

To fulfill your needs it would seem you'd need to hit up a landscaping company, which can charge so much for its presumably worthless dirt because of the supply-demand issue. You need it, they've got it, and no one else has it who's willing to give it to you cheaper.

Or is there?

Gather round, children, for there is an endless supply of free dirt that tends to be overlooked by most. You'll find all the dirt you'll need at construction sites. Whenever roads are widened or vacant land is being graded and improved, building crews and their mammoth machines stockpile massive piles of dirt in anthill-shaped mounds. The foreman won't like you messing with his construction site while he's got guys working, but he most likely won't mind if you check in after-hours with a truck—your own, rented, or borrowed—and a shovel to take it off his hands, since he'll need to pay to haul it away eventually anyway after his contract is up. And who will he pay to take his waste? The very landscaping company that was hoping to sell it to people like you, of course. If you don't break the chain by doing some sneaky, harmless trespassing and taking the dirt on your own, you can at least tell people that you did it to earn some street cred.

23. Yard Sale Hardball

Everyone knows that a good way to save money on household items is to hunt down garage sales. What garage sale shoppers don't quite comprehend is that, unlike most retail situations, they hold all the power. This might goes beyond the mere ability to bargain and knock a few bucks off the price. With the right timing and mind-set, you can walk away with nearly anything you want at a garage sale for either pennies on the dollar or for free.

For starters, never visit a garage sale before noon on Sundays. Saturdays are out completely, because buyers have a whole other day to sell their stuff, and thus aren't as desperate to get rid of it as soon as possible. Most people flood garage sales in the early morning hours, and usually on Saturdays, under the faulty assumption that they'll get the best stuff before anyone else gets a chance to look at it. At this point, the inventory is flush, the sellers are energetic, and the customers are in a competitive mode, looking to snatch up anything they can. Sure, the buyers can still talk the price down, but the sellers are much less likely to bend very far. Dollar signs are still in their eyes, and they're looking to maximize profit more than get rid of their junk. The nostalgia factor is still in play as well. When sellers watch customers poke and prod an item they've spent the last ten years with, there's an instinct to pull it out of their hands and stick it back in the garage. Good luck asking for less than the sticker price in such a scenario.

The early-hour and Saturday garage sale outings make sense only if you're a flea market vendor or eBay maniac looking for low-cost items to turn around and sell for a quick, easy profit. Anyone looking for things they actually need and plan to use should skip the early rush and sit back until garage sellers are just about ready to pack it in.

When the sales are winding down, all the power shifts into your hands. Late on Sundays, crowds have thinned out, sellers are exhausted, are sick of staring at their items that haven't yet sold, and just want an excuse to pack up shop. With this mentality, sellers are ready to give away everything they've got to whoever walks by. The alternative is to either haul it off to Goodwill, which is an annoying chore, or repack it into the garage or closet, which carries an air of defeat.

This, of course, is when you want to come in. You'd be surprised how much good stuff is still available at this stage, because it has either been overlooked by shoppers or was overpriced by the seller. To get the best deal possible, eye the object of your desire with a smirk, fiddle it around for a little bit, offer a laughably low-ball offer—say, $10 for a $100 TV—and if he shakes you off, walk away. If he doesn't chase you down and grudgingly agree to allow you to take it off his hands, he probably will a half hour later, when you return with the same or maybe slightly more generous bid. Another technique is to agree to a price higher than you're willing to pay—for instance, $25 for that TV—then dig through your wallet and pull out a $20 bill, explaining that it's all you've got. Once a seller thinks he's got a transaction in the bag, he's more likely to overcorrect any sign that it's about to fall through. For fear that you won't return, he'll probably give you your reduced price before you offer to drive away to retrieve more.

24. Cut the Cord

Cell phones are not a good deal. They're a heinous invention of the telecommunication industry geared to addict the public to their convenience, meanwhile ingeniously figuring out a way to throw out the one-phone-per-household business model in favor of a one-phone-per-person standard. Not only that, but every person now pays at least $50 a month rather than $30 for a landline.

With all this in mind, my advice is to still get a cell phone. The depressing fact is you need them in modern society. I held out as long as possible myself but finally submitted to "the call" in 2004 when I missed out on a chance to interview Quentin Tarantino because I was stuck at my girlfriend's sister's wedding a hundred miles away from home. Missing the chance to talk to one of my greatest heroes felt like having ten puppies die at the same time. The next weekend I trudged to a Verizon mall stand and signed up for the cheapest plan I could find. I was soon as addicted as everyone else.

For more than a year I kept my landline, mostly out of habit. I'd grown up with one and couldn't fathom life without it any more than I could without a TV or microwave. I hardly ever used my regular phone, and yet I dished out $30 a month to Qwest. I'd sate myself with little rationalizations that cell phones were unreliable, so I needed to keep a landline if I ever needed to call 911, or the thought that I may get over the Tarantino debacle, ditch the cell, and return to the previous way of life. Also, I needed the landline if I were to continue my cheap, dial-up Internet service, and also if I ever gave in to the TiVo siren song. Constantly staring me in the face was the unacknowledged realization that I needed to get rid of the landline, although doing so would make me feel like I was walking around without underwear.

I finally cut the cord after I'd upgraded to a cable Internet connection and came to the realization that my old, clunky VCR was a suitable substitution for my TiVo pipe dream. It was worrisome yet gratifying to call and disconnect my phone service, but I haven't missed the phone once since I boxed it up and plunked it in the garage. I've been to many weddings since, cell phone in pocket. Alas, Tarantino has yet to give me another call.

25. Worldwide Walkie-Talkie

Tear up all your calling cards and rip those 10-10-WHATEVER stickers off your landline phones. I know a couple ways to subvert the system of high-cost long-distance charges, and I'm not heading into a computer voiceover Internet protocol (VOIP) praise like those Skype infomercials that come on at 6 AM every morning. By the way, I have a message for the stalker-boyfriend in those infomercials who lives in California and travels to Asia and gets Skype so he can keep calling his girlfriend who's away at college in Texas without having to pay long distance: Your girlfriend is totally cheating on you, dude. No matter how many times you call her over the Internet, you're not going to be able to stop her from upgrading over your sorry ass. Everyone sees this but you, but guess what— you may as well stay in that worthless long-distance relationship because you know you'll never be able to do any better.

Ahem, so back to the subject at hand: how to avoid paying for long distance. My first tip is to whittle down the information you're trying to deliver into a three-second sound bite, make a collect call, then rush to give as much info as possible in that brief window the operator leaves for you to say your name. Example: If you want to tell your grandmother in Amsterdam you've earned a promotion, say "HigrammaitsJakeIgotabetterjob." If you need to tell Uncle Henry in New Zealand you've been accepted to med school, say "Stanfordjustacceptedmeyaysendmoney." It may sometimes take a few calls to relay your entire message.

For instance, you may start with a phone call with "Hidadmy girlfriendspregnant," and follow up a couple minutes later with "butdontworryitsprobablynotmine." You can make as many calls as you like, and whomever you're calling can do the same in returning your messages.

Although I opened this portion by speaking dismissively of VOIP, bear in mind it's only the pay services I look down upon. I'm fully supportive of squeezing every ounce of value possible out of your overpriced monthly broadband fee. E-mail and instant messaging are wise communication alternatives, but sometimes you just want to do the voice thing. That's where VOIP comes in.

I brim with anger that VOIP calling was once free, just as many dial-up Internet service providers such as Juno or NetZero once provided free dial-up, before the consolidation demons ate away much of what was great about the World Wide Web. Now all regular VOIP plans seem to be pay services that charge at least as much as landlines, but there is an alternative, and it comes in the form of video games.

My cheapest VOIP solution is to buy a regular Nintendo DS online for about $100—that's $30 cheaper than the redesigned DS Lite—along with one of the DS games that provides voice chat, such as "Metroid Prime Hunters," "Tony Hawk's Downhill Jam," or one of the Pokemon titles. You can find a used copy of one of the games for less than $20. Next, tell your friend in a far-off land to make the same purchase. Now you can hook up any time and talk as long as you want to without ever having to pay a monthly fee, thanks to Nintendo's free WiFi network.

Your one-time start-up fee has netted you a lifetime of free conversation and will pay for itself in less than six months. You don't have to worry about keeping track of minutes, and you can also shoot each other's virtual heads off if you ever run out of things to talk about. If only we could convince everyone to get a DS, we could put Qwest out of business.

Sony's PSP is a slightly pricier option, but the newer models of the Sony handhelds let you use Skype, which is free when you're talking to other Skype users.

26. F U I DON'T TXT

As if the punishing monthly call plan costs for cell phones weren't enough, the mobile communication industry has also built in several extra ways to soak you for not only your arm and leg, but your kidney and half of your left lung, too. The most nefarious of these is the minute count, a scheme that makes you either buy more minutes than you'll need or overpay for any extra talk time above your monthly threshold.

The onus is on the consumer to do everything he can to cut down on minutes. Thus the likes of Verizon and AT&T are forcing everyone to behave like a jerk, dismissing small talk in order to rush to the meat of the conversation, interrupting one another, and hanging up without saying goodbye. Behaving this way is, of course, highly recommended by me, as is screening all calls in order to determine whether or not they're worth answering, then rarely returning any of your messages.

Yet even these practices aren't always enough to keep your minutes down, because your phone conspires in your undoing, much like the robots in *The Matrix* who have enslaved humanity. You'll notice that the counter on your call timer starts when you place the call. No one ever picks up on the first ring you hear from your end because the ring has inserted an electronic buffer as your call is being patched through. The person on the other end of the line doesn't hear a ring until the caller hears the second or third, and thus several extra seconds have been added to your conversation before it begins.

The time-wasting travesty is even more pronounced whenever you're leaving someone a voice message. The windy default message goes: "The person you are about to reach at the number 555-555-5555 is not available. If you'd like to leave your callback number, press 1. Or hold until the tone to leave a voice message."

The whole "callback number" spiel is useless due to caller ID and exists solely to stretch out your phone time. There is almost no way to get through this nonsense without having your message take up more than a minute, and if your message seeps even one second into that next minute, you get dinged for the entire minute.

So what can you do about it? Never leave voice messages. Hang up as soon as your call goes to voice mail. The people you're calling will still be able to see that you've phoned if they check their missed-call log.

Downloading ring tones is also a bad idea, and the same goes for games or mobile Internet. Anything you'd use your cell phone's meager Internet function for other than e-mail—such as stock quotes, movie times, sports scores, and news headlines—can be found for free on 1-800-555-TELL.

Also, stay away from text messaging; a practice that makes no sense because it's so labor-intensive and costly—at 5 to 25 cents a message (they even make you pay just to read a text that's sent to you!) or $10 a month for unlimited messaging. A call to your service provider can get texts blocked from your phone.

I never text, and no one who's in love with texting has ever been able to explain its validity to me. They always just laugh and say they're addicted to it. Those who rationalize texting by saying it's a way they can talk to people without bugging those whom they're with are full of it. There's no bigger distraction than some idiot sending dumb, misspelled love notes to his girl-friend while he's at a baseball game with his pals. Those who say texting provides privacy are also misinformed, since text mes-sages are all saved in a cache by your provider, and manuscripts have been admitted in court as evidence on countless occasions. Also, anyone—especially a cheated-on significant other—can grab your phone and scroll through your history.

My conclusion to the reason for the texting phenomenon is that the act removes an extra layer of intimacy and perceived intrusion. If your text message isn't returned immediately, it's not as official of a rejection as a missed call, since it can conceiv-ably be returned later. People are too afraid of being brushed off and dismissed, so they use texting as a pathetic, impervious shell for their insecurities. Be bold. When you need to talk to someone, make a phone call, and never open or respond to a text message.

27. Death from Above

Bugs are such dicks. They think they can roam around your house with impunity, eating your food, gnawing holes through your walls, and hiding in your shoes so they can bite your toes. Try and stand up to these tyrants via chemical warfare and you're not only hurting the insects but also yourself. As cruel as bugs are, weeds are even meaner. They sprout up out of nowhere and strangle cute, innocent little flowers to death by stealing away all the soil's nutrients. They ruin lawns and uglify front yards, multiplying like horny jackrabbits and driving down property values as much as a corner crack house. Weeds are so darned stubborn and mighty, they'll even bust through your concrete.

The sneaky, insurgent-like attack methods of bugs and weeds are so intimidating that you may be afraid to fight them, preferring to cut and run and cower in fear on your couch. But fear not, I say! Take the fight to the bugs and weeds so you don't have to fight them in your own home.

Chemical warfare WMDs such as Raid or Roundup only spread toxins around your home, which is a side effect that might be worth tolerating if these bug-killers didn't deplete your defense budget.

Your savior, dear reader, is piss and vinegar. And by "piss," I mean soap and water. The liquid solutions are the respective kryptonite and death ray of insects and weeds.

Keep a spray bottle filled with diluted dish soap on hand, then blast ants to oblivion whenever they rear their stupid, antenna-poking faces anywhere near you. One spray and you can rain death-fire upon an entire squadron. The ants will be in so much pain, their ant spirits will float back to the anthill and warn the children to uproot and move to Hawaii. The effect of watching 10 billion ants collectively clutch their balls in agony after they've been soaped up is so gratifying, you'll practically be begging ants to invade your yard just for the chance to kill them. I'm telling ya, you'll be planting half-eaten cupcakes and bird carcasses every ten yards in order to dare other ants to step up and take a smack down.

Soap kills ants because ants are dirt bags, and soap murders dirt. Soapy water murders ants so hard, it actually makes weeds laugh.

But those weeds will stop laughing once you bust out your vinegar.

Take a jar of vinegar—a good way to get vinegar, by the way, is to ask if you can borrow some from the neighbor, then use 90 percent of it and refill the jar with water like you used to do with dad's vodka so it looks like you didn't use much—and flood it all over every weed you ever see. Vinegar is a sadistic bastard of an herbicide bomber, so do your best to keep it away from the good plants. Of course, any plant that's near a weed is reasonably accusable of harboring a weed, and thus equally culpable for its crimes. Vinegar busts a cap in thistles, crabgrass, and dandelions, then comes inside to kick your ass at Madden on Xbox 360. Trust me, don't ever mess with vinegar. Do your best to stay on its good side.

28. Hang Yourself Out to Dry

Every house, and most apartments, shelters a demon. This demon disguises itself as a kindly appliance that only works to your betterment, but don't trust it for a second because the moment you turn your back on it, the demon ratchets up your electric bill, chews up your socks, and kills your kittens. There was once a time this demon didn't exist, but technology paved the way for its prominence.

Of course I am referring to the electric dryer.

Sure, you may think you need this fire-breathing beast. But brother, fire ain't free—nor are all the garments you've accidentally shrunk to the point of ruination by subjecting them to the infernal, size-reducing breath. As for the pieces of clothing you've outright lost to the dryer, don't think for a moment that you really either misplaced them or let them slip behind or under the washer. The dryer has devoured your socks and underwear, having accepted them as idolatrous sacrifices to appease its evil nature.

If there's one thing dryers take pleasure in destroying more than socks, it's money. Ever accidentally wash and dry a dollar bill? It's bunched up like a fifth-grade spit wad and is just as valuable. Money laundering, indeed.

If you know what's right for you, you'll take an oaken stake or silver bullet to your dryer, destroying it before it can wreak any more havoc on your finances. Failing such drastic measures, at least sell it in the want ads or at least disconnect it and just use it as a shelf. You may miss your dryer at first, but after a couple weeks of air-drying you'll be glad you've done away with it. Hanging clothes on racks outside not only costs less than drying them electronically, it also gives them a fresher scent, a comforting, air-dried crackle, and never subjects your threads to shrinkage. My favorite dryer alternative is the $7 collapsible plastic drying rack I bought at Target. Because I live in a hot climate, my stuff dries quicker outside than it would in a dryer anyway.

This antidryer advice goes double for those who use laundromats. You'll save so many quarters by air-drying that you'll be able to build your own Scrooge McDuck money bin, passing your wealthy days by swimming and diving through a sea of coinage.

Finance

A finance chapter is a no-brainer in a book about saving money, right? The way you handle your money can be as important as how you spend it. Lesson one: Don't stick it under a mattress, because the only interest it will collect there will be paid in bedbug feces. The financial world is a shell game filled with sharks and marks. Your job is to make sure you're the former.

29. Work over Banks Like a Loan Shark

In olden times you'd need to be a loan shark to aim for 75 percent interest on your pocket cash. And even then you'd need to pay part of your commission to a brass-knuckle-laden heavy to collect it for you. Not so in the modern banking world, which is rife with competition for your checking-account patronage.

Check your mailbox any day of the year and you're likely to get one of those offers for an opening deposit bonus if you open an account with direct deposit. Some banks require you to bring the mailing in with you to collect your reward, while others don't even care and will hand over the bonus cash to anyone with or without a pulse. Most offers require a minimum opening deposit of around $100, but don't sweat the figure, since after you set up your account you can immediately walk outside to the branch's ATM and pull your money back out. I always keep a single penny in there just to avoid exposing myself and risking that the bank will close out my account and demand its money back. The bank tags your account with a couple easily avoidable catches: It requires that you keep your account open from six months to a year or else you forfeit the opening bonus and it will charge you a monthly fee in any thirty-day span in which a direct deposit isn't wired. There's also a waiting period of about a week until the bank gives you the promised money. The banker will also probably try to slip in an order for checks for you, which you should always decline unless you don't mind a $13 fee for checks you'll never use. The new account starter kit includes five or six free dummy checks anyway, and you'll only ever need to use three of them, max, and all three will be addressed to yourself: one to take back your opening $100, one to swipe away your bonus cash, and a final check to clean out your account once your account has been open long enough to avoid a penalty.

The toughest part of maintaining a dummy account like this for the requisite amount of time is gathering up the nerve to set up a direct deposit for $1 every two weeks. In my younger days, I'd sheepishly bump up the amount to $50 or $75, then withdraw the money and move it back into my main account, but this was all too much work just to keep up appearances. I mean, what's so important in impressing the HR lady? It's all about me, and I want to start up my accounts and forget about them, so the direct deposits need be the absolute minimum so I'll never miss the money. For instance, an account open for six months with a $1 direct deposit every pay period will only take $13 out of your pocket in the entire span. When it's time to close the account, that $13.01 you withdraw seems like free money. So these days I proudly march into the HR cave with my $1 direct deposit start slip, and the lady is so used to helping me do what I do, she keeps my file on top of all the others, like what Mr. Belding used to do with Zack Morris's permanent record. I try to keep a healthy rotation of six or seven accounts open at any time, and when I close one out I'm sure to open a new one at the same bank a couple weeks after. This nets me an extra $600–$700 a year.

30. I'll Take All the Credit

Credit-card companies are sneaky little bastards, luring you in with eye-dilating promises only to sock you sideways with astronomical interest when you least expect it. The cards offer silly handouts such as frequent-flier miles, gift cards, and cash back as high as 5 percent on certain types of purchases because the financiers in charge know that if they get enough fish to bite, most of them will be stupid enough to gulp down the hidden hook rather than nibble away the lure.

Don't be a gulper. Be the prototypical enemy of the credit-card industry who keeps CEOs awake at night. Buy everything you can with your credit card, pay off your balance every month, and jump through all the proper flaming hoops in order to collect your rewards as quickly as possible. Living on an all-credit-card, all-the-time lifestyle is a little dangerous, but it's a good dangerous, like Mel Gibson in the *Lethal Weapon* flicks. The benefits include getting back a tiny portion of the cash-money society pries out of your cold hands with a crowbar, allowing you to shift all your resources into savings and investments rather than keep cash on hand to handle day-to-day expenses, as well as the peace of mind of never needing to monitor how much spending money you've got left before making a purchase.

Bear in mind that it takes a consumer of a certain discipline to thrive on the credit-card lifestyle—one who remembers every purchase is made with real money even though it's real money that exists only in electronic code readable on a magnetic strip on a brightly colored plastic rectangle. If you've got the funds in savings—preferably in a 5 percent annual percentage yield account such as Emigrantdirect.com—to match everything you buy on credit, and if you don't spend any more than you normally would if you were paying in paper, you'll win and win big.

Any slipup, though, meaning a late payment, can undo months of accomplishments. A nasty interest rate and late fee charges can eat away much of your winnings.

Your first step should be to cancel any credit cards that don't give you monthly freebies, then divert all your spending power into one special card you'll always keep at your side. Start by searching online for a reputable Visa or MasterCard issuer that will give you a tasty bonus just for opening an account, such as a $50 gift card. Next, find ways to put all your bills on the card, although be careful to avoid companies that charge you an extra fee for credit-card bill pay. Never, ever, be shy about using your credit card, even in seemingly ridiculous situations such as a 99 cent double cheeseburger purchase at McDonald's. The free money adds up as long as you stick religiously to your plan. To maximize your benefits, always offer to be the guy who pays in collective situations such as office gifts, group meals, sporting events, bar tabs, business trip hotel rooms, and the like. Pull out your credit card and take everyone else's cash. Folks will usually overpay for fear of looking like cheapskates, and you can keep the extra money without needing to be concerned about requests for change.

31. Mysurvey.com, Mypoints, My Money for Nothing

A certain rule about Internet moneymaking schemes: For every ten thousand Nigerian bankers, work-from-home offers, and chain letters declaring that Microsoft will send you $10,000 in the mail if you forward the message to everyone in your address book, there is one valid fund source. And no, I'm not talking Google ads, which will make you about a penny per year unless you're lucky enough to sell your blog to Gawker, in which case Gawker will get the penny per year from Google.

The real money-for-nothing over the Internet doesn't come in floods but in microbursts. Subject yourself to an amount of steady tedium and you'll be able to scrap your way to a miniscule, semisteady paycheck.

My favorite source for easy, albeit slow, e-money is Mysurvey .com, which bombards you with marketing questionnaires and compensates you very minimally for your participation. The service has a point system set up that awards you a set amount depending on the time it supposedly takes you to complete the task. Once you get 1,000 points, you can enter a raffle, get a menial prize, or, my favorite, order up a $10 check.

These surveys could take hours to hack through, but I just turn off my brain and randomly click on every answer in order to get through the surveys as quickly as possible. On average I get a few surveys a month and earn a $10 check two or three times a year. I accumulate a large sum of my points through referrals. In the fine tradition of pyramid schemes, you get 150 points for each person you convince to sign up for Mysurvey. This means I don't want any of you to register for the site on your own. Send me an e-mail and I'll refer you.

It may not seem like it's worth it to plow through time-wasting surveys for such a minimal reward, but doing things like this is my idea of fun, so no worries. With your approval, Mysurvey will also send you samples and mail surveys that are accompanied with $1 or $5 bills. The best is when you meet the right demographics for a survey that sends out samples to you. I'm still using a bottle of shampoo I got a year ago, and I was sent a VHS screener of the *Prison Break* pilot episode months before it aired. Membership, I say, has its privileges.

To a lesser degree, Mypoints.com is another winner. Sign up at this site and you consent to having yourself spammed with hundreds of e-mails a month from companies making boring, not-so-special offers to you. In my three years with Mypoints, not once have I come across a promotion that was even remotely appealing. No matter, you don't have to take the companies up on any of their deals—you just have to show proof that you've subjected yourself to the pitches. Click on a button embedded in each e-mail to prove that you've read it, and you get 5 points. Once you accumulate 1,000 to 1,500 points, you can score a restaurant gift card. I usually go with Olive Garden. I only get one or two of these a year, and I probably waste eleven hours or so going through all my Mypoints spam, but I'm just demented like that. If you are too, please allow me to refer you and collect 100 points per head. The site only gives you credit for five referrals a month, so you'll have to wait your turn.

32. This Must Be What It Feels Like to Be a Slot Machine

Every so often, your local Indian casino will put out a free match-cash coupon, meaning if you bring the ad to the gambling establishment, you'll instantly double your money before your first bet. The coupons are usually branded with a $5 denomination, although I've seen them as high as $20. You can get the same offer if you sign up for the casino's players club, but that's just a one-time thing since they take your driver's license or social security number and bind it to your account.

When casinos do a mail-out or newspaper promotion offering these little slips of paper gold, it's as though you're a slot machine, collecting all kinds of cash while falsely promising that you'll spit out more than you take in.

Whenever I open my mailbox and come across one of these gems, I instantly abandon all my plans and start traveling to every community mailbox in the city—with a premium on those with a giant trash can close by, usually at apartment complexes—and dig through the discarded junk mail with the rootin' tootin' giddiness of Yosemite Sam once he thinks he's discovered a lost gold mine. No matter that some of the coupons are smeared with rotten banana peels or used condoms. I just peel off the nastiness and pocket them. Once I've got my stack secured, I jam them into my car cup holder and get ready for two to three weeks of money-grabbing fun. You'll stop only when the coupons expire or your stash runs out.

Each day after work, I head down to the casino with three or four coupons, then make it a skill game not to beat the dealer in blackjack but to covertly sneak around every corner of the casino, cashing as many coupons as possible without being spotted and thrown out for violating the fine-print rule that you can only redeem one such coupon a day. If you're wary of the eye in the sky, make it a point to get to the casino at 11:50 PM, and trade in one coupon before midnight and one after in order to cut down on your gas consumption and time wasting.

Most casino attendants will give you the cash straight up, but some are hard-asses who only pony up once you've stuck your $5 in a machine. This is fine, just go through the motion, let the attendant insert the matching $5, then cash out right in front of him. If you feel the need, you can even make a comment that this machine doesn't feel lucky to you. The moneyman will buy the excuse because all gamblers are superstitious loons.

I look to cut down on gas expenses by recruiting a friend whenever I've got more coupons than I can possibly use. I give one or two per trip to a pal who drives in exchange— overpayment, to be sure, but these are coupons I wouldn't be able to use anyway—and make it a tag-team effort. Operating with a buddy is even more fun than violating the casino's rules on your own. You feel like the guys in *Ocean's Eleven*, only you're content with taking home $20 instead of $150 million. And you don't get to bang Angelina Jolie like Brad Pitt does, or every hot woman on earth like George Clooney does. And your witty banter isn't as funny. But you get the idea.

33. It's in the Cars

Car dealers just love to mess with you. Their training involves a laundry list of bush league psyche-out ploys meant to bend you to their will and become money-spewing putty in their sweaty, trembling-from-stress hands. Dealerships are intimidating places, what with the high-pressure sales tactics, the huge sums of cash trading hands, and the tense negotiations for everything from interest rates to floor mats. The dealers are counting on nerves clouding your judgment as soon as you step through the doors.

Be aware, however, that it's really the dealer who should be intimidated, because he's the one with everything to lose. It's as though you're locked up in a poker match and you're the one with the big stack and the nuts, while he's got a pair of twos and needs to bluff his way into making you fold.

The way to break a dealer down and get him working for you, instead of the other way around, is to turn some of his tactics on him.

Dealers always try to get on your good side, either by gladhanding or pretending they're letting you in on some insider information, such as when they pull out an MSRP sheet in the guise of showing you the so-called lowest price available. The dealer wants you to think the MSRP is the price they paid for the car, but be aware that it's actually an inflated price with a standard markup to give the dealer a profit margin. The dealer wants to insinuate that it's the rock-bottom figure, but the truth is dealers can, and will, sell their inventory for far less than they paid for it in order to clear out old models and meet sales quotas. If you pay MSRP, you're most likely selling yourself short.

Another ruse car salesmen pull is keeping you waiting. The idea is that the longer you spend in his office, the more committed you'll feel to finishing the deal in order not to feel as though you wasted time. He'll run off to "talk to his manager," meaning he's just sitting alone behind closed doors, waiting ten minutes to tick off before he rushes back in with some sort of great new deal, just as you're ready to give up and leave. You can pull a reversal on him by waiting patiently, then having a friend call you on your cell phone and insisting you need to take this call, and then making *him* wait for fifteen minutes. Or you can just go to the bathroom and read for a while, just to get him as irritated as you would be if you weren't onto his game.

Never be afraid to walk out on a deal, even if you've already handed over your down payment check and the boys in the back are detailing the new car you're about to buy. Even if you're getting a great offer and the dealer is complying with your every wish, never close a sale until you've walked out and he's dragged you back in with a slightly sweeter bargain, maybe a $100 rebate or free oil changes for six months. If the guy doesn't follow you, that's probably a sign that he won't bend anymore. Does this mean you should turn around and buy the car? Not at all. Now you know the best deal this particular seller can offer, and you can take that knowledge to a rival dealership to use as a bargaining chip. If Dealer 2 can't beat the offer, it's back to Dealer 1 the next morning.

34. Drive Me Crazy

The fun to be had at car dealerships doesn't stop in the negotiation room. One of life's great pleasures comes in the quasi-scandalous test-drive deals offered most often by cheesy used-car dealerships willing to do anything to drag people onto the lot, even if it involves giving away stuff such as TVs, trips to Vegas, or cash (or involves outright lying).

I enjoy responding to every test-drive giveaway I see. In my days I've found that 75 percent of these offers are genuine, while the other quarter are just as rewarding because they allow you to alert the local media or tattle on them to the Better Business Bureau. The one constant in all these promotions is that the salesmen despise them because they draw people to the dealerships who aren't looking to buy a car but are more interested in wasting the sales staff's time en route to getting something for free.

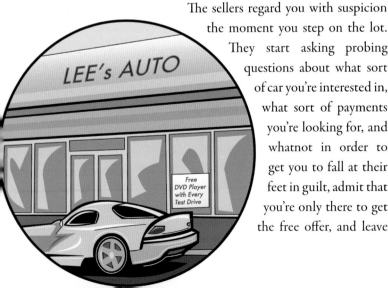

The sellers regard you with suspicion the moment you step on the lot. They start asking probing questions about what sort of car you're interested in, what sort of payments you're looking for, and whatnot in order to get you to fall at their feet in guilt, admit that you're only there to get the free offer, and leave in a hissy fit. My style is to play it free and loose, going along pretending that I'm actually interested in whatever car I'm taking around the block, then telling them it's too expensive and I'm not ready to buy a new vehicle after all just yet. And by the way, when do I get to step into the swirling money chamber I saw in the commercial and grab all the $1 bills I can shove in my pockets in forty-five seconds?

The dealer will never freely offer you the promotional item, because it's best for the business if you just walk away empty handed. When you ask for your promised portable DVD player after your test drive, the salesman usually calls your bluff and asks you if that's the only reason you came. I always reply in the affirmative, and the disgruntled guy, feeling burned that he's squandered his best pitch on a loser with no intention of lining his pockets with a commission, drops his fake grin and barks back, "You should have just told me, man. We wouldn't have needed to waste all that time and I just could have given it to you."

This is a complete lie, which I know for two reasons: One, I've actually tried to skip the test drive by just asking for the promo straight out on several occasions, and I've been immediately asked to leave by the manager every time. Two, a friend of mine used to work at a car lot, and he tells me salesmen get a small commission for each test drive they can get a customer to take. No way will the guy turn anyone down who wants to take a test drive. I think they lie to me because they want me to give myself away, but I don't fall for it. When the salesman tells me I should have been honest with him, I just snap back, "Pleasure doing business with you. See you next time you guys do something like this."

35. Show Me the Money

This next trick will earn you $20 extra out of the blue, and though it may seem silly, it's worth doing because twenty bucks is twenty bucks. Wait until you're seated at a table closing a car or house loan, at the point when the loan officer or seller is hunched on the other side of the table, completely sure he's long since closed you and is now just waiting for you to put pen to paper and make it official.

This is when you lay your pen on the table and declare that you need $20 or you'll back out. You'll probably get laughs, followed by jeers and accusations of insanity. Bear in mind that you don't exactly have to use the $20 figure. You can just as easily gun for $50 or $100, but there's something magical about $20. Most importantly, nearly everyone always carries at least $20 on them at all times in case of an emergency, and the easy access to that which will satisfy you makes it all the more compelling for the financier to grant your silly wish. It's large enough to be worth trying for, yet small enough for your opponent to willingly part with without feeling bad enough about the manipulation to tear up the paperwork and send you on your way based solely on principle.

One time when I asked for $20 at the loan closing, the finance guy accused me of nickel-and-diming him, to which I agreed.

"Four hundred nickels, actually, or two hundred dimes, or whatever you prefer. But one $20 bill will work also."

With tens of thousands of dollars for the business and hundreds of dollars in commissions for the closer on the line, he won't be willing to let a sale slip away over a matter of just twenty beans. He may hem and haw, try to dissuade you, or distract you with counteroffers, such as a gas card or voucher for a free detailing or window tinting, but stick firm to your $20. If pressed, just explain that you like the house/vehicle and you really want to buy it, but it will take $20 to make you truly happy with the deal. Tell him it doesn't matter if he deducts it from the loan amount—which he'll never do, by the way, because doing so will force him to print up all new paperwork—or just give you the cash right there. If he says he doesn't have $20 on him, which is almost certainly a lie, tell him you'll wait until he goes and withdraws the cash from the ATM. I've found he'll usually just shake his head, pull out his wallet, and slap the $20 on the table. Part of the pleasure of doing this, actually, is getting to witness the passive-aggressive acts of contrition through which you get your cash. One time I had a particularly disgruntled loan dude wad up his $20 and throw it at me as I was walking out on the deal. I thanked him, signed the paperwork, and drove off in my new car.

36. The Pacman Effect

One of my greatest heroes is Pacman. Here is a guy who knows what he wants and goes after it at full speed, with mouth wide open, ready to devour all he sees that is good, and to run with abandon from everything that's out to get him. Gordon Gekko from Wall Street, the guy who said, "Greed is good," is an amateur compared to Pacman. I need to make myself a set of bracelets, bumper stickers, and T-shirts that read WWPD, which stands for "What Would Pacman Do?" If I asked myself this question in more phases of life, I feel I'd be a much more happy and successful man. I'd also be a whole lot fatter, but that would be a small price to pay for my wealth and accomplishments garnered through living in the Pacman way.

What Pacman knows is that contrary to the maxim, there is no such thing as too much of a good thing. Well, maybe there is if you eat too many cannoli in one sitting, but certainly not when you're talking about power pellets or money. When you find something advantageous in the wide world of money, take advantage of it over and over again until you're eaten by a regenerating ghost or physically forced to stop.

This piece of advice holds true as an enhancer for every other suggestion in this book, but it's especially applicable when it comes to loose change or coupons that put change back in your pocket, and are thus just as good.

Whenever I see a coin, coupon, or ticket on the ground, I pick it up without a thought. It doesn't matter to me how dirty, gum-crusted, or trampled-on it looks, nor does it matter if it's only a penny. The way I see it is since the planet looks for every way possible to shake me down for another penny, I may as well collect the pennies and nickels that spurt forth from the ground to even out the difference. Many folks raise their eyebrows or shake their heads in derision when they see me halt my course to pick up a penny, but I just brush aside their condescension and think: "WWPD."

Does Pacman care that the micropellets in his haunted labyrinths carry a negligible point value, especially when compared to the bouncing watermelons, cherries, and pretzels that are worth so much more? Hell no. He chomps every damn thing with the same fervor, knowing full well he won't be satisfied or allowed to get to the next level until he's eaten absolutely everything there is to be eaten in his current line of sight.

This is truly a mentality to live by.

To better understand my point, try to think in the long term rather than the short term. A person who goes through life ignoring stray change will end up considerably poorer than one who grabs every penny, dollar bill, and dime he can get his hands on. It all adds up, and I'd venture to guess that a guy like me will end up with $5,000 in found change by the time my life is over. The converse is the dude who doesn't pick up change is basically throwing $5,000 away for no reason. What a moron.

The fact is, people who don't brake for pennies or nickels are hypocrites. Everyone has their price—you can't tell me there's a person alive who wouldn't stop in their tracks to scoop up a $100 bill on the ground—it's just that they've arbitrarily raised their standards. You, me, and Pacman know that all money is money, and the lower the standards you have, the greater your rewards shall be.

37. Fool's Gold

Name your cliché: Discretion is the better part of valor, fools rush in where angels fear to tread, and all that glitters is not gold. Those like us—and I'm assuming you're like me if you've made it this far into the book—are particularly susceptible to pouncing on deals that seem beneficial at first glance but actually turn out to be either—at best, far more trouble than they're actually worth or, at worst, outright frauds that can cost you more than you'd ever let your greedy, get-rich-quick-scheme-blinded mind fathom.

This is one of the most important chapters in the book, because for anyone to save money, they have to avoid giving it away to scam artists. If you don't follow the advice in these couple of pages, there's not much else I can do to help you, for you are a "fool and his money who are destined to be parted."

The idea, of course, is to stay away from bad deals that appear to be good deals. With that in mind, here are some rules of dumb ruses to avoid at all costs (I regret to admit to gaining much of the following knowledge first- or secondhand):

- Pyramid schemes. Whenever a supposed "friend" asks you to dinner for a "business meeting," then proceeds to go into a bug-eyed, grinning explanation of some life-changing, direct-selling business that has changed his life forever, get out of there. Don't even stay to hear him out or laugh in his face. These things can run you into the ground, sapping your savings in exchange for products unable to be sold, and forcing you to rope in everyone who's close to you to sign up just so you can get out of the red.

- Infomercials. If it's on TV in a paid advertisement on a triple-digit channel at 6 AM, it's not the secret key to becoming a billionaire. No real estate instruction videos, franchise opportunities, or stock tips are worth ordering from a 1-900 number. In fact, the only good ideas you can get from watching this junk is to start an infomercial of your own and sell something just as bogus to TV-glued morons. This advice doesn't apply to the infomercials with the dude who sells prayer cloths that will make all your wishes come true. Dude's totally legit.

- When the mullet-haired guy pounds on your door and says, "Hey, I got a hundred top sirloin steaks in my van! I'll sell you some for five dollars each!" just slam the door. No good has ever come from buying frozen meat out of the back of some guy's roadside vehicle.

- Scientology. It isn't as good a deal as it seems. Let those Thetans (volcano demons that make you think bad thoughts) stay inside of you, because it'll cost far more counseling sessions than you can afford to be as peaceful as John Travolta.

- Zero-down loans. Unless your interest rate is zero percent, a nothing-down loan is a good way to stay on the rental treadmill for a few more years. If you don't start with a down payment, that means practically everything you're paying toward your mortgage or auto loan is going toward interest for several years. You're better off hitting up a rent-to-own place for your furniture.

- Cash-advance joints. Think about it—if you're really so hard up that you can't get any more cash advances from your credit cards, will you really be able to spare $500 from your next paycheck fourteen days from now? The answer is no, and these shysters who run the ubiquitous, scourge-of-society, cash-advance joints know it. They're counting on you to default and drift into the 500 percent interest written in the fine print of your contract. Give plasma, pawn your TV, or sell your arm to science. Whatever it takes.

38. Don't Poop on Coupons

An old roommate used to make fun of me for clipping coupons on Sunday mornings as I watched football. He considered it feminine. He was completely wrong, of course. There's nothing more masculine than hunting the wild prey of elusive offers that will slash sizable sums off your monthly grocery bill. And my protests fell on deaf ears.

It saddens me that coupon clipping is viewed as the pastime of the desperate housewife, some meaningless, mundane project to fill the time between soap-opera airings, floor mopping, and self-supplied, amateur porn web-camming. Here and now I want to start an effort to reclaim coupon clipping for men everywhere. I want Harley riders to start keeping plastic, accordion-style coupon holders in the back of their hogs. I want UFC fighters to tout the benefits of $1 off Raisin Bran coupons after bouts. I want John Wayne to rise from the grave, visit a Circle K, and push a buy-one-get-one-free Thirstbuster card over the counter.

Coupons are real money, and to throw them away is to ignite your wallet in flames. Granted, they're also a marketing scheme to trick you into favoring name brands over generics, or buying more of something than you normally would, but as long as you don't alter your purchasing strategy, you can't go wrong.

Sunday morning paper circulars are the best source to fill your local coupon stash. It blows my mind how Sunday paper circulation is plummeting around the country, because the coupons contained inside pay for the cost of the paper infinite times over. It's a marketing problem, really. Publishers should simply forsake the tired concept of news on the front page in favor of 200-point headlines that scream BUY ME AND I'LL SAVE A DOLLAR OFF YOUR CORNFLAKES, $4 OFF YOUR DR. SCHOLL'S, AND $10 OFF YOUR TEETH WHITENER.

Traditional papers are only the beginning of your coupon safari. Make it a regular practice to visit the home page of any business or manufacturer for online deals, which often come in printout-coupon form, and hit up Web-based coupon clearinghouses, including the aptly named Coupons.com, for a regular look at their wares.

Some undertapped coupon resources include ghetto community weeklies, kid-aimed publications, and, my pride and joy,

student handbooks handed out on campus at the beginning of every college semester.

On the first day of classes, I make a triumphant return to my alma mater, the University of Arizona, with my backpack strapped on, ready to cruise the student union breezeways to pocket the sundry student coupon books that line desks propped up by the walls. Businesses recognize that lots of college students are hard up for cash, so they'll cut them deals they hold back from the rest of the world. About once a year I'll find a deal that's insanely good, such as a free personal pan pizza, $5 in casino money, or a 99-cent meal at the cafeteria.

While I'm piling entire cases of these coupon books into my backpack—once in a while I just take cardboard boxes in which they're contained and march them back to my car—sometimes the pang of guilt hits me, and I wonder whether I'm unfairly stealing good deals from starving college kids who need the savings far more than I do. Then I wipe the thought out of my head, reasoning that I'm actually helping with their education. If I weren't there, they'd have no way to learn that they need to get to these coupons as soon as they can before some creepy townie takes them away. It's a valuable lesson, and they should be grateful I'm not charging them tuition.

39. Keep on Walking

I'm pretty sure that whoever was responsible for planning out the locations of your bank's ATMs took great pains to track your daily routine in order to ensure that none of their machines would be placed in convenient spots for you. Meanwhile, your rival banks conducted similar research and placed their ATMs exactly where you wish your own bank's machines were. This vast conspiracy is in place to get you to do something you should never even consider—pay exorbitant ATM fees. You may not miss the automatic charge of a few bucks when you take cash from an ATM that belongs to another bank, but crunch the numbers and you'll be ashamed of yourself. Not only does your own bank hit you up with a charge when you stray beyond the usual network but so does the bank that owns the machine. On top of that, the business at which the machine is placed in front of also likes to add in its own fee. The result is that you may often find $4 or more offered up as virgin sacrifice just so you can get your hands on a $20 bill you already own. That's a usurious 20 percent interest rate, and every bit as stupid as telling your boss you refuse to be paid for one of the five days you work each week.

The obvious way to skip ATM fees is to altogether avoid ATMs, or at least those from outside your banking network. Alternatives include trips inside the brick-and-mortar buildings to withdraw your cash the old-school way or visits to convenience stores that let you use the cash-back debit option. Cash-backing it can get a little hairy, though, since you'll need to make a purchase to get your extra money, often something you don't need, and if it's at a convenience store, that something will always be overpriced. Also, some of these franchised corner stores add a fee of their own onto your withdrawal.

There are more creative alternatives, however. One is to keep a checkbook on hand so you can borrow money from people in a pinch, then write them a check for the amount and have them feel as though you're paying them back immediately. With any luck they'll misplace the check and you'll skate. I also advise using your debit or credit card whenever possible, avoiding cash altogether. Always check, especially at mom-and-pop places, whether you'll get an extra fee jacked from you if you use your card. When you're making a sizable purchase, you should back out of the sale at the last moment unless they agree to drop the fee. All businesses pay a percentage of their credit-card-bought sales to the credit-card companies, and they should either absorb the costs themselves as a reasonable investment for the increased business credit-card acceptance gives them or not accept the cards altogether. Business owners will comply more often than not, because the prospect of having to put back all the stuff on the shelves isn't worth the extra dollar they'd collect from you.

40. Bank of Best Buddy

One of the best ways to get free money is to rely on your friends and family for loans, then avoid repaying them until weeks or months later, or, better yet, wipe out your debt in bets or bartering.

If you happen to have a pal who's a gambling addict, you're in luck. Just borrow freely from the guy and bet him on trivial things again and again, going double-or-nothing until he loses, which, as his bookies and favorite casinos know, will eventually happen. Be the house, not the player. Your friend will comply, unlike a rational person, because the dollar signs in his eyes will blot out all sense of reason, and all he'll be thinking of is increasing the amount of imaginary money you'll pay him back instead of the cold reality that you never plan on making good.

If you're unfortunate enough to be stuck in a friend circle lacking a degenerate gambler, you can turn to the ancient method of trade to rectify your deficit. In college I used to lend money to Magill who was far more successful with the women than I was. I once let him out of $40 he owed me if he agreed to hook me up with four girls. He happily agreed, and I promptly deleted his IOU from my mental ledger. The fact that he never came through for me with the dating help didn't mean that he owed me the money again. Well played, Magill.

Other friends will agree to not have you pay back their cash if you let them punch you in the face or give them a coveted item, such as an old Star Wars action figure or maybe a hard-to-find DVD. You should always offer up these things freely, because over the years he'll likely forget how he came into them anyway, and you can just ask for them back, insisting you only lent them to him.

Other go-to barters include giving the owner rides, running errands, making or buying meals, washing cars, or doing things around the house. Always make sure that your action will cancel out your debt completely before agreeing to comply, lest you fall into the Seinfeldian trap of having to buy someone lunch to pay them back for giving you a suit when it's actually dinner they were expecting. And never lend the suit to Kramer.

41. Juice Doesn't Taste So Good

I've tried to stray from the tried, true, beaten-in-your-head-until-it's-black-and-blue advice in this book, and this portion, in which I preach the value of paying down your debt and investing in your 401(k), may seem like it doesn't belong in such an unorthodox book. Not so, I declare, because so few people actually live by this mentality. It's so much easier and seemingly logical to avoid looking at the larger picture in favor of spending all your money on immediate pleasures. Only true bad-asses make themselves suffer today so they can relax tomorrow.

It all goes back to the old fable of the grasshopper and the ant your momma used to tell you when she was rocking you to sleep. If I remember right, there was this dumb-ass ant who used to waste his days by spending all his money on hookers and candy canes, while the studious grasshopper paid off his mortgage and bought a Honda Accord instead of a Trans-Am in order to sock away funds for his retirement. The pompous, self-righteous grasshopper tried to force his mentality onto the stubborn, lazy ant, but they finally agreed to stop bickering and work together once the entire yard was sprayed down with pesticide. Then along came winter, and the ant died of a heroin overdose while the grasshopper keeled over from internal bleeding brought on by the ulcer he inflicted on himself through his neurotic lifestyle. The moral of the study is that one in the hand is worth two in the bush, meaning only you can prevent forest fires.

Sooo, while that fable might not have taught you anything and only worked to contribute to your juvenile delinquency, my message for you is much clearer: Treat debt like the crabs, taking whatever pains necessary to eliminate it as soon as possible, and take your employer up on all its perks even though doing so will mean accepting a lower take-home paycheck. It may sound overly strict, but it's all about punishing yourself like the OCD grasshopper so you can live like the hard-partying ant once you're old enough to know not to do heroin.

This world is divided up into two classes of people—those who struggle their whole lives to fight off the juice and those who make the juice flow toward them, and in turn get everywhere they want to go by coasting along with the flow.

The ideal is to transform yourself from the former class to the latter by making the juice work for you. That means focusing your entire being on getting rid of any and all debt that you have. Making extra payments on your student, car, and house loans is the surest, most lucrative investment you can ever make. People like to go around bragging they made this and that percentage on the stock market, but they're oblivious to the fact that their real gain is much smaller than they imagine, or possibly nonexistent, because they fail to take into account the interest rates on their debt. Example: Someone who made 5 percent on $10,000 invested in stocks for a year profited $500, but if the 10 Gs had been used to plug away at their $100,000 mortgage with a 7.5 percent interest rate, they would have actually knocked an additional $750 off their principal, which would have in turn lowered the overall interest they paid that year and would go on to need to pay the rest of the loan term. Complicated math made simple: The investor would have done better if he took $249 and made a bonfire. So always make it your first priority to get rid of your debt, and if any naysayer tells you it's okay to carry a mortgage because the interest is a tax shelter, you have my permission to sock them in the stomach because they're rationalizing and exaggerating the miniscule tax savings, especially if they take the standard deduction.

A tougher pill for most people to swallow than funneling extra cash toward their loan payments is sacking up and paying into the retirement plan. Let me preface by declaring I never want to retire, and, in fact, I think retirement is for losers, as is the prospect of socking away money in your youth just so you can afford a better country club when you're old and feeble. I advocate redirecting money into your 401(k) because it's a way to screw your employer out of the most money. If you don't sign up for these programs, you're leaving money on the table. Pay in as much as your company will match, and even if you quit or get fired and cash out, suffering the early withdrawal penalty, you'll still profit a healthy percentage. For instance, if your company matches dollar for dollar, you'll come out at least 50 percent ahead after the government takes its nasty cut, simply because you were smart enough to take the free money.

42. Bank Off

When you notice an extra charge on your bank statement, think of it not as a cut-in-stone loss but as the opening offer in a negotiation. Or better yet, think of it as a little prank pulled by a witless organization that must be joking if it actually thinks it's in any position to charge you for nothing and still retain your business.

In the Internet age, it's most definitely a customer's market as far as checking accounts are concerned, and banks will do anything short of fetching your newspaper and slippers in the morning in order to stay on your good side. Banks can make you read all the fine-print policy pamphlets and sign all the disclosure contracts it likes, but in the end, you will nearly always be able to get your way so long as you're liberal with the threat of taking your business elsewhere. I have a perfect record of getting every overdraft fee, ATM charge, check purchase deduction, and transaction fee rebated to my accounts. All it takes to remain fee-free is persistence and a short temper. It's in your best interest to get even a charge as small as $2 wiped off your account, because doing so will help keep your dossier clean. When the call-center supervisor takes a look at your record, you always want him to see that you've never been charged a fee, and thus must be a solid, reliable customer undeserving of being screwed this time.

You can finesse the complaint phone calls all you like, but it all boils down to a simple script:

Bank: "Hi."

You: "Take off my charge."

Bank: "Why?"

You: "Because it's not fair. Take it off."

Bank: "No."

You: "Give me your supervisor."

Supervisor: "We won't take off the charge."

You: "I'm closing my account then."

Supervisor: "We'll take the charge off."

Things usually won't even advance that far, but keep in mind that you're always holding the trump card. It's in the bank's best interest to keep you on the account docket and give back your measly $2 because it figures it will be able to bilk thousands of dollars out of you over your lifetime if you're kept happy enough to go to the bank for loans, second mortgages, and credit cards. The checking-account fee schedule is a smaller moneymaker for banks, meant to exploit dumb, passive customers who get confused easily and won't think to stand up for themselves.

43. Rebate Mania

It's really important that you master rebates. Say "master rebates" three times in a row real quick. Get it? Ah, tough crowd.

Moronic jokes aside, my point is that you should master rebates in order to avoid the consumer pitfall of paying more than you planned for something. Manufacturers bank on the expectation that a sizable percentage of buyers will be hooked by the sweetheart cash-back deals they post in ads, then not follow through on the rebate function. It's a good bet from their end. Always put your money on society's ignorance and laziness. People buy their new camera, get home, and lose the receipt, or they decide it's not worth their time to fill out the paperwork, cut the UPC code off the box, and mail in the self-addressed stamped envelope, only to wait eight weeks or more for a check that may or may not come. The rebate-offering business throws up so many obstacles in front of you to subconsciously convince you it's too much trouble.

The bonus for the company is it doesn't need to actually lower the price in order to bask in the benefits of its pseudo-sale. Because a certain percentage of customers will never call them on their promised rebate check bluff, they can make the rebates even larger. Pretend money is a lot easier to give away than real green.

Once again, the Sunday paper is your friend when scouting for rebates, although a call to customer service will do the job just as well. Electronics chains such as Best Buy tend to offer some dandies, which can slice 25 percent or more off your purchase price. Occasionally there are even offers that actually give stuff away once you factor in the rebate discount. I've picked up a DVD rack, a memory card, and a cable modem thanks to such bizarre deals.

Precision, record keeping, and hounding are the keys to receiving your rebate. Read every word of the rebate terms and conditions before filling out your form, because mess anything up and you're forfeiting the money you've got coming. Use your best handwriting, because you don't want to allow the rebate company the "cop-out" that your form is illegible. Most important, make copies of everything you send, including the bar code, rebate form, and guidelines. Mark the expected return date down on your day planner or PDA, and call the 1-800 number if they're even a day late with your check. Failing your initial ignorance and laziness, businesses are also hoping that you forgot you sent your rebate form altogether, and it's important you bombard them with phone calls until they follow through. Once your little check comes in the mail, all your diligence will be well worth it.

Oddly, online purchases seem to include a lot fewer rebate offers, probably because sellers expect online customers, who are already dealing with the mail to get their stuff, have no problem jumping through more mail hoops to save money. Or maybe it's just that online customers expect e-rebates, and the e-tailers aren't about to offer them because they're so easy to cash in over the Internet. You'll want to stay with terrestrial purchases if you want to milk the rebate cow.

44. Hospital Bill Amputation

My firstborn, Luke, was born in 2007 with a sticker price of exactly $330. My second-born, Emma, came in 2009 and soaked me for $3,000.

Even though Emma's birth was far more expensive, due to a crappier health plan, it would have been a whole lot worse had I not convinced the hospital and doctors to knock $1,000 off the bills.

I wish I could tell you I pulled out the deal with crafty demands, dogged persistence, and a threatening letter-writing campaign, but here is how the "negotiations" actually went:

Me: "Hey, my friend told me that if I offer to pay the bill in full over the phone, I get a 25 percent discount."

Billing department dude: "Okay."

And just like that, I was able to make my mortgage for another month. That first call was made based on what I thought was crazy advice from my wife—who is always collecting silly, usually inaccurate rumors off stay-at-home mom message boards that I refer to as "young wives' tales." But lo and behold, it actually worked! It seems the medical establishment is so used to getting stiffed by patients who either declare bankruptcy or just flat-out refuse to pay, that they'll give up one in the bush for three in the hand.

Overjoyed at getting $600 slashed off my hospital bill, I was certain the tactic would only apply to hospitals, which are so beaten down by losses from illegal immigrants and homeless people that they're desperate for any cash they can get their hands on. But sure enough, it worked on each of the myriad medical professionals that came out of the woodwork to hassle us for money. I got the obstetrician, anesthesiologist, and pediatrician to hack 25 percent off their admittedly inflated bills. ($20 for a box of facial tissue? Come on!)

The phenomenon actually made me look forward to getting new bills, just so I could negotiate them down with my new secret magic trick. As soon as I was done making my rounds, of course I immediately called up the hospital and obstetrician to get them to cough up the $82.50 I overpaid back in 2007, but unfortunately that didn't work out so well. It seems the whole asking for the 25 percent discount thing doesn't work out so well when you hold no leverage and the doctor has your money.

Money may not be everything, but timing certainly is.

Leisure and Entertainment

WASHINGTON

My favorite analogy for entertainment comes from the video game *Grand Theft Auto: Vice City*. When you step inside a strip club in the game, the indicator at the top of your screen showing how much money you've got left steadily declines. Such is the case with most any worthwhile amusement. Lucky for you I've got some hints that will stretch your entertainment dollar. Sadly, however, I've got no advice on how to save money inside video-game strip clubs. But face it, those pixel strippers really know how to work it, and watching them is worth every virtual dollar.

45. Renew Schmenew

So help me, if I ever hear of you renewing a magazine or newspaper subscription from this day forward, I will find out where you live and smack you upside the head with the book you're holding right now. Another business tactic relying on customers' laziness, as well as their gullibility, the renewal is a sadistic prank played on you by the publishers of your favorite rags. They operate like my elementary school crack dealer, figuring that since he's got you hooked, he may as well nudge the price up bit by bit, hoping you won't notice or question his methods in your blind lust for your next hit, um, issue.

What they don't want you to know is you will always be able to find cheaper deals online—offers meant for new subscribers only.

Moreover, they treat you like an old husband does his wife of several decades. He no longer brings her flowers or takes her out dancing because he figures he's got her in the bag and sees no reason to woo her. Don't be that neglected wife. Show the magazines that they still need to romanticize you and show you a good time if they expect you to put out.

Thus, when you try to renew online, you're swept over into a higher-priced renewal area. This is why you don't actually renew online, but simply use the Internet to scope out the lowball cost of your publication of choice, keeping the knowledge in mind when you call to negotiate your renewal rate. Print publication customer service types are coached to be as passive and accommodating as possible and work to avoid your cancellation at all costs. I subscribe to four magazines: *Game Informer*, *Sports Illustrated*, *Maxim*, and *Newsweek*. Every time one of them has come up for renewal, I've used the Internet-and-phone-call method to get the online rate without any hassle. Many times I've also gotten the special gifts offered only to first-time subscribers, hence my plethora of *Sports Illustrated* swag, including T-shirts, jackets, and, yes, tucked somewhere in the dark recesses of my garage is the football phone. If the customer service rep ever does give you guff, insisting that whatever offer you're going for is only for noobs, counter that you're fine with that and will simply cancel your subscription and call back the next day as a new subscriber. Feel free to add an "oh, snap!" afterward. The exclamation will be well-warranted because you've trapped them in their own hypocrisy and will surely get your way. Bonus points if you get them to respond, "You sunk my battleship."

Let me backtrack a bit and advise that before you start up a new subscription, always take full advantage of the trial period. The "bill me later" option on those irritating subscription card inserts is a valuable asset. You can receive a month or more of your magazine for free, then cancel and start up a prepaid subscription—magazine companies usually won't let you get away with the trial period thing again and again—never having had to pay for the issues you've already received.

46. Everyone's a Critic

If my time as a film critic has taught me anything, it's that security guards at the vast majority of press screenings don't care who they let into the theater. Ninety percent of the time, I would just say I'm a reviewer who works for the newspaper and the guy lets me in without even looking up at me or even glancing at the sheet with the names of people who are to be allowed in. It seems just the knowledge that there is a screening is all you need to be able to not only peep movies for free but see them before the general public. Compared to the ability to sneak into screenings, those $2 pirated copies of flicks that guys on the street sell out of the back of their Yugos are bad deals.

A little background: For most major releases, movie studios rent out theaters a few nights before release day to hold advance showings with the hope of spreading word of mouth and gauging audience reaction. It may seem counterintuitive to let audiences see the films for free, but it makes sense because most of the people who show up at these things are too cheap to buy regular tickets to movies anyway.

To defray the rental and security costs, the likes of Disney, Sony, and Warner Bros. will have their marketing guys sell sponsorships to local media outlets, who give out tickets to their employees, advertisers, and customers. If you've ever heard the guy on the radio going, "OK, caller number nine who says the phrase that pays gets a chance to see the new Cool FM special premiere of the latest *Spider-Man*!" you know exactly what I'm talking about. Because the radio station shells out the money, its obnoxious morning show DJ gets to hold court before the screening, run his tired shtick, toss out T-shirts, and promote his program.

These screenings usually start at 7 PM and can occur any night of the week, but Tuesday nights are the sweet spot in which there's almost always a screening going on. These nights are reserved for the biggest film opening that week and are the prime slots because they give reviewers time to crank out their reviews and get them in print by opening day without allowing them enough time to reconsider their rushed opinions and backtrack, or worse, let them have weeks to spew their hatred of the films all over the blogosphere.

All the studio cares about is getting rear ends in seats, and that's where you come in. It's convenient to get to know the screening reps, who will give you passes and clue you in on screenings, but flak ass kissing isn't at all necessary. Just show up at 6:30 any Tuesday night, bringing along a notebook for good measure, and act as if you belong in the theater. Confidence is everything. Act all nervous and suspicious and you're giving them a reason to question whether you belong. Deflect any questions about your veracity by making up some publication, radio station, or blog you work for and walk into the theater in a huff before they think to grab you by the shoulder and send you out. You can even bring a date along, because press members are allowed to take a guest to each screening.

47. Discount Double Feature

This technically illegal but widely accepted rite of teenage film geekdom can serve you well until your death. You know the drill: Buy a ticket for an early show, preferably a matinee, and hop from theater to theater, taking in all the cinematic bliss you can handle in one outing until your stamina or conscience catches up with you. When caught and asked for your ticket stub, either mumble and head for the nearest exit or pretend you're lost and don't realize you were sneaking into another movie.

Some see it as their God-given right to bounce from film to film without tediously stepping outside to purchase a new ticket, because admission prices are so high and the theater setup is practically begging you to exploit it, what with a multiplex hallway of unguarded doors bubbling with the silver screen excitement within. Those people can go ahead and move onto the next segment because you're every bit as unscrupulous as I am and you don't need to be talked into anything. The other group is convinced that seeing two or three films on one ticket price is the same as stealing. This faction is not altogether wrong, but they aren't as on the mark as they think they are.

To understand my point, look at things from the business' point of view. There is a raging moral debate about whether or not it's okay to theater hop, and you should base the decision on who your sympathies coincide with. Movie studios are aghast at the thought that you'll stay to see their film after buying a ticket to one of the others which it's trying to beat in the weekend box office race. Meanwhile, my guess is the theater manager could really care less what you do while you're in his building, so long as you're not peeing on the floor in one of his bathrooms. He figures the more time you spend in the house, the more likely you are to make him rich by visiting the concession stand to buy some of his exponentially marked-up popcorn, candy, and soft drinks. The snack counter is where the theater sees most of its profit. Ticket sales are mostly commandeered by the studio. For opening weekend films, in fact—which are what makes up for most of the business anyway—the theater pockets less than 10 percent of your ticket price. That's probably why the manager makes it so easy for you to stay and catch another flick. If he made you buy another ticket, his multiplex would only see another dollar, and take $10 more out of your pocket that would be better spent on food, which lets him see a profit of 90 percent or greater. Whatever resistance his ushers put up against your theater-hopping is only token, to convince the studios he's running a legitimate operation. If the theater is bustling with customers, there's not much motivation to hustle moviegoers out the door when the shows are over.

So by paying for a movie at 11 AM, watching four or five movies and not leaving until 11 PM, you're really doing the theater a favor, provided you fill up on the overpriced, movie-time goodies.

But if you're a bastard like me who sneaks his own food and drink into the theater, you have no redeeming qualities. And I'm pleased to make your acquaintance, my brother.

48. Cheapest Seat in the House

One way to combat the rising cost of tickets to sporting events is to avoid paying altogether. How do you do this? By going to the stadium way early.

This is a little something I picked up in my time as a sportswriter. I'd neurotically get to the game hours in advance to do my pregame reporting and when I'd get there I'd find almost no one else at the arena. Even when there were people there they'd just greet me with a nod or casual "hi," never asking to see identification or even ask me for justification of why I was there. The press box and clubhouse would be locked, but I'd have free rein to wander wherever I liked. I made a mental note at that time that whenever I wanted to see a sold-out game, all I needed to do was get there superearly, hang out, get a few hours of reading in, then blend in with the incoming crowd and eventually set up camp at the seat of a no-show.

Four or five hours before a game is set to begin (maybe twice as long before a football game), the doors and gates are unlocked so the athletes, media, and support personnel can go in and out as they please as they scurry to get the event underway. The reasoning is that no sane person not paid to be at a two-hour basketball game so long before it starts will actually show up so early. Anyone who does show up so early must have a legit reason. Security guards won't even get to most games until, at the earliest, three hours before kickoff/tipoff/faceoff/whatever-other-offs there may be.

The great thing about this mode of sneaking into sporting events is there's probably nothing illegal about it, since most stadiums are publicly funded and you're technically just using a public facility, then happening to stay there as walls of security form around you. Sure, several arenas are on private property, and even if you're asked to leave at a public place by a team official you've got no right to stay, but as long as you're not making an issue of yourself, you should be able to slide. It's true that you're pulling a scam, but you certainly haven't committed an egregious offense, such as counterfeiting a ticket or slugging the usher in the stomach while you run in. Besides, if the game is sold out, you're not even keeping any cash out of the coffers, since the team already maxed out its sales figures. The only people you're hurting are the scalpers, who deserve the hurting.

In addition to the thrill of the sneakiness, there's a certain aesthetic pleasure to arriving at a sports game so long before the event. If you're a big enough sports fan to sacrifice your whole day just for one game, there's no doubt you'll appreciate watching the grounds crew get the field ready, the administrative staff making their frantic preparations, and the athletes walking in wearing street clothes and headphones. It's all prologue to the main event that can't be matched even by tailgating and talk radio chatter.

49. Flask Attack

I'm pretty sure I got this one from a movie, and if not, my friend Tim certainly did. Whenever he goes out to the clubs, he always keeps a tin flask filled with vodka inside his coat pocket. This guy is a genius. Not only did it save him money, it also allowed him to get wasted on the cheap while he used his saved cash for higher purposes such as buying women drinks and taking a cab ride home. Tim's method also surpasses other time-tested bar savings endeavors such as drinking at home before driving out to the bars—a major DUI risk—and stopping by the grocery store to pick up a 12-pack, then guzzling beers out in the parking lot before getting in line, which is just begging for getting busted for drinking out-side. The flask is stylish and efficient; slick and easily concealable. The flask is a James Bond—like tool, sort of the invisible remote-controlled Aston Martin of the drinking-scape. No one has to know you're flaskin' it unless you feel like sharing the knowledge with them.

At first, Tim's friends ridiculed him as a cheapskate for

bringing his flask out to drinking establishments every weekend. But he persevered, as steadfastly devoted to his cause as Frodo. Like Galileo, he was persecuted only for being ahead of his time. At first it was only Tim using the flask, then it was Tim and Glen. Eventually the momentum shifted and Tim sat back idly like Gregory Peck in *Twelve Angry Men*, confident that he'd enacted sweeping change through self-satisfied perseverance.

To get maximum return out of your flax, buy as cheap a drink as possible, or better yet, order a cup of ice water, then discreetly liquor up your drink, keeping it at the same level throughout the night until the entire contents of your container are now pumping through your blood and bladder, spurring you onto the brave idiocy only liquid courage can provide.

A small side note: I'm not a drinker because alcohol makes me sleepy instead of happy, and I can't justify paying for the privilege of making my eyes bloodshot. The best and safest way to enjoy the nightlife is to go out without pounding drinks. Call yourself the designated driver, or whatever else you need to do to stay sober. Since everyone around you is inebriated, you have your excuse to behave like as much of an idiot as you feel. And there are few more entertaining pleasures in life than being a sober person talking to a drunk.

50. VIP Entrance

L as Vegas—it's the land of glitz and glamour. One of the only deals worse than the roulette wheel is the $500-an-hour call girl. And the only deals more raw than the hooker are the exorbitant cover charges to get into the nightclubs. People line up for hours just for the right to dump $30 into the club's coffers in order to roam around a pitch-black, sausage-factory dance floor lined with cage dancers. Some bypass the lines by slipping the bouncers a Benjamin. And the drinks run $17, minimum.

I may not be able to help you with the roulette wheel, the whores, or the drink prices—except for that nifty flask idea —but the cover charge I *can* help you with. Use the rear entrance that exits into the casino, blending in with a group of hand-stamped revelers who are heading back into the club after a few rounds at the blackjack tables. The later in the evening you try this, the better chance you have at success. By late, I actually mean early. These places stay open until four in the morning, so you'll actually do better if you're a superearly riser, hitting the sack early and setting your alarm for 2 AM, when the security guards are glazed over and the defenses are more penetrable. Don't fret about missing the 10 PM–2 AM club hours, because nothing goes on during that time anyway, and if you head out that early you'll spend hundreds buying drinks for ladies until they're inebriated enough to view you as attractive. Better to skip the preamble, let some other dipshit get your lady liquored up, then swoop in as the closer once she's ready to leave.

Once you've made it into the club, you can get your hand stamped on the way out and be golden for the rest of the night, stepping out to gamble and circling back in as often as you like. It's not a terrible idea to play a few hands at the table, slurp down some comped drinks, then head back onto the dance floor buzzed enough to think you can bust some sexy moves. You can gamble that $30 cover charge and possibly parlay it into some more cash. If you lose, don't fret—you were playing with money that actually should have belonged to the casino anyway.

By the way, I was lying earlier when I said I couldn't help you with the prostitute. A friend tells me of the time in Thailand he and a pal invited ladies of the night from a massage parlor to their adjoining hotel rooms. My friend allowed his escort to complete her end of the transaction, then was shocked when she received a text message from her friend, the other prostitute, informing her that the client refused to pay. This ignited my friend's date into a hissy fit, which he quelled by phoning security to have the two girls kicked out of the hotel, allowing my friend to get off, quite literally, without paying. Mind you, this took place in a third world country and not Las Vegas, so it wouldn't be advisable to try in a land where American tourists are not valued above the locals. Also, my normally impervious friend felt deep pangs of regret afterward. "I hope there's no hell," he told me, "because if there is, I'm going to it."

51. Trial Without Error

Here we shall discuss two tenets of mail-in movie rental program exploitation: the trial period and the corporate rate. Combine these and you conjure an unbeatable combination of free movies delivered to your home. Follow my advice and you can see all the movies you want for free for the first five or six months of a year, then, if you choose, watch movies for a discounted price the rest of the year before starting the entire process over again.

Start off by jotting down all the movies and TV shows you've always wanted to see but have never made the time for. The size of your list determines how long you'll need to ride the program out. If you're at all like me, you'll come up with a depressingly long list that you won't be able to put a dent in if you continuously stared at your TV in this lifetime and the next, and that's completely fine. What I'm teaching you can be used and reused in perpetuity.

Next, cull together whatever DVD mail-in rental programs you can find—Netflix and Blockbuster, to start with. Scope out each of these rental programs, sizing up what sort of free trial periods they have, then start with the first service, using your home address and favorite credit card to sign up.

Next, get to watching your movies as quickly as possible after they arrive and·send them back so you can prepare for the next set. If you're lucky enough to live in an area in which your mail is delivered in the morning or early afternoon, you can call in sick when your movies are due, watch all three in succession, then race them to the nearest post office before the last pickup of the day.

Act diligently enough and you can motor through fifteen or more movies in your trial period. Once it expires, simply cancel and move onto the next service, and when that trial period is up you switch over to the next one. Do some homework and you can find six or seven of these, meaning you'll be covered well into the third month. Once you've exhausted all your trials, start over with the first service, this time switching to your work address and a backup credit card in order to sidestep the one-trial-per-household-per-year standard that seems to go along with most of these programs. With the right timing, you'll have made it through nearly the first half of the year without once paying a membership fee.

Once you're this far in, you're most likely addicted to your ingrained sofa spud lifestyle and because the more you see the more you realize how much is out there that you *haven't* seen, your list will be even longer than it was when you started, so you'll need to make an arrangement to tide you over until you'll be able to qualify for the next round of free trials.

This is when you give up your freedom and subscribe to one of the online rental places but only the one that offers you the quickest turnaround and is willing to cut you a deal. Call around and beg each place for a corporate rate, never mind that you're undeserving because your job doesn't involve watching DVDs until your TV melts down. You'll almost always get what you're asking for, shaving anywhere from 10 to 25 percent off the standard rate. Just be courteous and polite, and the call center folks will hook you up. What do they care? It's just another subscription to chalk up on their commission chart, and the business lets them do what they want because they know that even with your reduced rate, they're still overcharging you anyway.

52. Hotel Dress-down

Clothes not only make the man, but they make others' impressions of the bloke. Imagine coming across a beggar who is dressed in Armani—you wouldn't even think of tossing the guy a buck and would be more likely to laugh at him. People are making constant judgments about who you are, what you're like, and, most important for our purposes, how much you're capable of paying. Rarely does this spur-of-the-moment evaluation come more into play than when checking into a hotel.

Make yourself look a little poorer than normal and there's a hefty chance the desk clerk will give you a lower rate. March in with a briefcase, suit, and slicked-back hair and you're more likely to be sized up as a business tripper susceptible to being overcharged, oblivious to smacking down an extra $40 a night because it's going on your expense account. Also, if you appear desperate, as though this hotel is your only possible respite for the night, you're asking to pay the maximum allowable by law.

It should go without saying that when traveling with a group, always keep the others in the car while you check in solo. Double-occupancy rooms trigger a naturally higher rate, so you always want to appear as though you're alone. Once you've checked in, you can always bring the others into your room without much of a problem—if you're confronted, you can just say that they're friends in town who are dropping by for a visit.

More preliminary advice: Unless you're traveling to a smallish town during the one weekend of the year all its hotel rooms are booked for a convention, eschew reservations. Prebookings in the usual situation, in which there are ample rooms available, only serve the hotel and lock you down into the highest rate it can charge you (leaving no room for negotiation). You want to arrive in the hotel unattached, after dinner but before midnight, willing to move onto the place next door if you're not happy with what a room costs at one joint.

Pretty much, the later you check in the better. Late in the evening, hotel managers have resigned themselves to the fact that their take for the night is pretty much set, and any extra customers they can draw in at that point are just gravy. If you seem wealthy and committed to booking a room at his place, the manager may still milk you for all you're worth, and that's why you've got to grunge yourself up.

Make it a point to forget everything mama taught you about dressing nice and making yourself presentable. Don't let a comb come within twenty feet of your hair, draw your clothes from the laundry basket and under your bed rather than the closet, and skip shaving for a couple days and bypass your shower and deodorant rituals. You want to make yourself look as poor as possible without crossing over into maniacal drifter territory and be escorted out of the building by security.

53. Pay-Per-You

Once you've checked in for the night, it's time for some entertainment. How does a free movie sound?

Peruse the hotel's TV network of entertainment options, be they theatrical movies or spanktravision, then order one up regardless of the price. The morning you're checking out, call the front desk and claim that your film cut out halfway through. You'll instantly get the charge for the film taken off because, by calling so late, they won't be able to reasonably offer that you order the same film again for no additional charge. I recommend this particularly to business travelers who don't want to have a porno appear on the itemized bill they'll have to turn in to their bosses for reimbursement.

Who knows why this works? My guess is it has something to do with the general hotel pay-per-view movie system being somewhat glitchy, even though in my experience I've never had a movie cut out in the middle. The hotel is forced to take the customer at his word and has little to lose in providing a rebate since piping the movie into the room is done electronically—no desk man-hours or hotel resources were wasted. Hotels may as well advertise this perk on the marquee: ONE FREE PORN MOVIE PER STAY. Never mind that this policy doesn't make sense because who watches a porno all the way through anyway?

I first stumbled upon this phenomenon a few years ago in a trip to Las Vegas with my friend and his meathead younger brother, who worked for a national hotel chain at the time. We'll

call him Eddie, because that's his real name.

The room was under my name and credit card, and I was aghast to return from a night of gambling to find Eddie frantically covering himself in bedsheets to hide the fact that he was getting intimate with himself while provocative acts of sexual deviance were unfolding on the TV screen. As disgusted as I was by what he had done to the bedding, I had planned on sleeping in that night (let me pause here to offer a side note: If you're traveling with a bunch of guys and want to ensure you get a bed to yourself as the others voluntarily sleep on the floor, follow Eddie's example exactly). I was even more angered that he had charged a $8.99 porno to my account.

"Relax," he said. "I work for a hotel. You get one free movie."

I shook my head in disbelief, but the next morning he promptly rung up the front desk and put on a display of monetary magic that made up for the traumatizing event of the night before.

54. The Domino Scheme

Whoever invented the concept of taking turns for common purchases was an evil genius—a scumbag who wanted to make sure he got the most for the least, while whoever was with him got the least for the most.

The way to do this is to use rudimentary game theory—never offer to take the first turn, and always double up in the middle to create the image of generosity. For example, when you and a buddy are taking a long road trip, never be the first one to fill up the gas tank, otherwise you're putting yourself in a position in which there's a 50 percent chance you'll end up paying more in gas than your friend. And that means there's also a 50 percent chance you'll end up paying equal amounts, depending on whether the amount of fill-ups is odd—meaning you lose—or even—signaling a tie.

The first fill-up means everything because if you can get your friend to take it, that means you'll bump yourself up into a can't-lose position rather than a no-win. The way to get there is to play it cool, acting as if it doesn't matter. Maybe throw your wallet into the backseat when you start the trip, just so it takes longer to get to it than it would for your friend to pull out his credit card. Another way to clinch second position is to volunteer to pick up chips and a drink for your pal from the convenience store, rendering you out of the picture so he instinctively pays at the pump. By doing so you're also putting it inside your friend's head that he owes you a meal somewhere down the line.

The more I dwell on it, the more I convince myself that I could write an entire section on how to screw your traveling partners on road trips, but for the sake of succinctness I'll move on.

The gas-rotation paradigm works well with splitting bills and groceries with a roommate, dining out with other couples in a series of meals and carpooling to work. You can really use the system to romp your way to savings if your group is larger than two, however.

Say you're out to drinks with four friends. As you learned earlier, avoid responsibility of paying for the first couple rounds, then volunteer for the third, and then again on the fourth. You'll suddenly be seen as the most generous guy at the table, and the impression will hit all the more harder now that your pals are four drinks into their inebriated stupor. Meanwhile, guy No. 4 is viewed, probably accurately, as the cheapskate who has yet to pony up. Regardless of who pays for what the rest of the evening, your reputation as the generous one—and his as the cheap-ass—will stick, and as your binge grows longer and longer, you'll get off the hook while your friends badger the fourth guy harder and harder to step into the rotation out of turn. You're practically guaranteed to get two or three more drinks than you paid for.

When you're dealing with friends, you never want to act as if money is important, because if you're seen as the person who cares most about paying the least, you've stigmatized yourself and can no longer get away with anything. You always want to be the one they don't suspect or see coming. Those who appear to be generous can get away with being cheap more often than those who appear cheap.

My advice may sound Machiavellian, but really it's just a type of self-defense. For some reason financial turn-taking dominates our culture, and since taking turns sticks someone with a raw deal, it's simply responsible of you to avoid being the one who gets hosed. Don't be oblivious. Be a capitalist. The disgruntlement over a share-and-share-alike mentality is exactly why communism doesn't work. No matter how equal a concept may seem on its surface, there's always a built-in mechanism to exploit the worker and funnel the excess to the power elite. When you have a choice, always join the power elite.

55. Scalper to Scalp-ed

If you've got a date you want to impress by, say, not having her sneak into a sold-out sporting event six hours before it starts so you can avoid having to buy tickets, or if kids and parents are in tow, you'll want to go the scalper route. Never use eBay or any other Web site to buy scalped tickets early, because when time is on the side of the sellers, they can drill you every which way. You always want to wait until the day of the game, when these scummy entrepreneurs are most desperate, hanging out across the street from the stadium holding up placards declaring their position as resellers. These smug salesmen think they're taking advantage of folks like you by buying tickets early and marking them up for easy profit. Instead, your job is to make him do a service for you by having procured your seats early, then selling them to you for as much or even less than he paid for them.

Like meerkats and prostitutes, scalpers will stake out areas as their own, shooing competitors away with the stink eye in order to prevent competition and bidding, which are exactly what you want to generate.

You'll want to start making your scalper rounds an hour or so before the game is set to begin. It's true that by starting this late you'll miss out on the best seats, but by putting your quest off until the literal eleventh hour, you're also allowing others to weed out the worst deals. You want your vendor to be desperate and exhausted, his profit mark for the day already in the bag, just looking to clear out his remaining stock so he can head back to his lonely home.

Never accept a scalper's first offer. Approach the negotiation as a baseball player would an at-bat. Just sit there looking at the opening sucker pitch, and allow your opponent to toss a few junk offers your way, as well as a couple tempting strikes, before finally considering taking a swing. While you're arguing about the price, you should always say the guy on the other corner is willing to give you the seats cheaper, whether or not you've actually talked to him. This will force the scalper to at least hesitate, and possibly buckle under, before shaking you off. If he plays hardball, actually go to the other guy and use the first scalper's low price as the opening bid for whatever he's selling.

Failing all else, just wait it out. Disregard your need to get into the stadium before the game begins. The damn thing will last three hours, after all, so there's no rush. Allow game time to make the scalper skittish and more eager to get rid of his tickets, because he'll be aware that the value plum-mets with each passing minute. A nice line I like to use at the beginning of the game is, "You may as well give it to me for the price I want; oth-erwise I'm just going to wait out here with you until the third inning for you to sell it to me."

Scalpers are often fast-talking scam artists who are more skilled at closing deals than you are, but by bringing them down to your level you'll always get what you want. Brush off such excuses as whatever price he

56. Extra, Extra

Coffee shops are like pudgy, single women in their late twenties and thirties, or guys of any age or weight for that matter—they're so desperate for attention they're willing to give a lot of stuff away for free. They're painfully aware that the competition out there is stiff and unforgiving, so they'll do their best to earn your patronage by making you feel at home. That means plush chairs, stacks of newspapers and magazines, free Wi-Fi, and an accepting atmosphere with friendly employees who wouldn't think to shove you out the door even if you've been coming to the shop for a year and have yet to order even a single drink. This is especially true for local coffee shops, whose owners are paranoid that you'll stop hanging out at their place at the first sign of discomfort and make for the nearest Starbucks. And they should be. Starbucks is mighty accommodating and their efficient, customer-friendly business practices are the major part of the reason they've managed to snuff out so many mom-and-pop shops around the world while pushing caffeine to the point that it's become as lucrative an industry for South America as cocaine.

Starbucks is nice, but I would suggest choosing a local place to stake out as your home base, because the few remaining local shops will do even more to accommodate your slackery. You may find you can occasionally score free drinks, ordered up by a manager in hopes of getting you addicted, and some coffee shops even hold special events and offer door prizes.

Be cautious about regularly ordering expensive drinks because these can eat away at your profit center and cause you to fall into the trap set by the business. Remember, you want to become a squatter, not a customer. If you must order something to sip on, go for the small coffee, which is always the cheapest thing on the menu. (If the person behind the counter asks me, "Did you mean tall?" I say, "No, I meant small." I don't like to fall into their little name game crap. And I refuse to refer to the coffee makers as baristas because it's a dumb word. Begin accepting terms such as "tall" coffees and "baristas" into your natural vocabulary and you're a half step away from becoming one of those jackasses who pontificates online about malt mochachinos. Keep your sense of identity because you're attempting to bend the coffee shop to your lifestyle, and not the other way around.)

If you're armed with a laptop, you may be able to justify not needing to spring for an Internet service provider at home and can also consider canceling subscriptions to publications that are always lying around at the shop. If you've got a portable video-game machine such as a DS or PSP, you can use the shop for your all-night multiplayer benders.

Money-saving benefits aside, coffee shops are also good places to go to get work done and meet members of the opposite sex who are as lazy and flighty as you are.

57. Microsoft Point Shaving

Let me start by saying e-piracy in any form is just flat-out wrong. That said, there's nothing inherently wrong with downloading free games, so long as whoever created the games intended them to be free. And when the free stuff is as good as its expensive competition, which is often the case with old-school games, there's little reason to pay for downloads.

The seventh generation of video game consoles—the Xbox 360, PlayStation 3, and Wii—was the first to usher in the standard of downloadable retro games. Microsoft, Sony, and Nintendo backed into a collusion standard in which they and their third-party game publishing partners would charge between $5 and $10 to let gamers repurchase their youth game by game. Employing the ancient carnie and Laundromat trick of getting you to pay for more than you'll need by transferring your currency to a skewed system, Microsoft and Nintendo force you to buy redeemable points in preset numbers, making it so you'll always end up with a few points left over after you buy your games—just like how you always used to come home from the carnival with a few unused tickets. With your remaining Wii or Microsoft points—Sony actually plays this one straight, letting you transfer money directly into an online wallet—you're thus forced to eat the cost or pony up for more points so you can one day buy enough games to reduce your balance to zero.

The download phenomena replaced the paradigm of the higher customer value of the retro-roundup, in which publishers would pack ten to twenty-five old-school games on one disc and charge $30. Granted, gamers didn't get to choose which games were on the "classics" discs as they do with the current à la carte system, but there were most often enough games in the older packages to more than justify the price tag.

I believe the game manufacturers got too greedy with their inflated price tags and that all three systems would sell far more retro games if they lowered their prices to a more reasonable $2 or $3. By sticking with the $5 minimum, they've all but invited us to take part in the homebrew-led rage of free downloadable games.

Homebrew and its ilk are games for older systems made by enthusiastic geeks who emulated ancient coding and design in order to reproduce the games they love. The Internet is awash with Web sites that offer free homebrew downloads of nearly any game you can imagine. Game publishers decry homebrew as piracy, but their claims are rarely accurate, because homebrew games are usually close knockoffs rather than exact duplications. The big three video-game manufacturers are engaged in a constant war with hackers who break through console security systems, modifying them so they can play free homebrew games. Through online firmware updates, console manufacturers are known to permanently disable game systems modified to use homebrew games.

Don't mess with your newer consoles and simply opt for a modded Xbox or Dreamcast, both of which are available for purchase online for under $100, or just download games directly onto your computer and play them with a mouse and keyboard. If homebrew can remain strong through the years, maybe it will teach the video-game hegemony that they're losing out on business by sticking with higher prices and intimidation tactics.

58. I Feel Validated

When business reception desks put up those little signs that read PARKING VALIDATION FOR CUSTOMERS ONLY what they really mean is "Parking Validation for Customers, As Well as Badass Rebels Who Dare to Flout the System, Only."

Are you a badass rebel? I know I am, and that's why I get my parking validated wherever and whenever I see fit. Treat those signs, as well as surly parking guards who try to prevent you from attaining that magical stamp that wipes away that nasty parking garage fee, as nothing more than inconsequential jokes. An ounce of charm and a pound of perseverance can go a long way toward getting you to the Monopoly-like promised land of free parking.

Of course, the unguarded validation stamper is always the preferable route when set against a validator watched over by a human sentinel. A case study: Whenever I'm in Phoenix to catch a Diamondbacks game, I pull into the Arizona Center parking garage a few blocks away and insist I'm there to see a movie in order to avoid paying the $5 flat fee for baseball parking. The Arizona Center is a run-of-the-mill, open-air mall with a movie theater, a few restaurants, and a crazy flag shop that sells confederate banners to the truly disturbed. Once I've finished with my game, I head for the theater, which provides four hours' worth of validation—perfect for a baseball game— and tell the ticket taker that I just got done watching a movie but forgot to get my parking card validated. So many people go in and out of that theater that they're in no position to doubt me, so I'm allowed right in to hit the automatic stamp before I go off on my way. Only once did the guy actually ask me what movie I had seen, and I instinctively responded, "The one with Ben Stiller." You can never go wrong with this reply, because there's always at least one movie with Ben Stiller in theaters at all times. It's like a rule.

Things can get a tad trickier when you have no movie theater–like option and have to confront a stingy restaurant, bank, or business in order to get your validation. I avoid smallish mom-and-pop shops whenever possible because these places are run by burned-out characters who throw their all into their jobs, know every one of their seven customers by name, and don't take too kindly to strangers out to step into their joint only for a parking ticket hit-it and quit-it. Go for a chain restaurant and ask one of those nice hostess girls if she'll run in and validate your ticket. If they ask you if you're a paying customer, just say yes. Make it easy on them and don't force them into any confusing moral dilemmas. You're better off sticking with kindly youngsters rather than grizzled, bottom-line-oriented managers whenever possible.

Failing all else, you can go with the punchout method, which is

KANANI'S HAWAIIAN CUISINE

Parking Validated
for Customers Only

best suited for daredevils and only doable if you've got an accomplice with you. Wait until late in the evening when you're sure no cars are arriving, then drive up to the entrance, leaving yourself an escape route in case an oncoming car makes an appearance. Have your pal hop the blockage arm and punch the ticket dispenser, causing the arm to rise up. You'll have just enough time to scoot your car to freedom, then make it to the outlet street before pulling over to let your wingman back in the car. I recommend driving slowly because it isn't worth risking an accident to save a few dollars. Well, it is worth *risking* an accident; it just isn't worth actually getting into one.

59. Bump Me Baby One More Time

On one of my favorite Web sites, Consumerist.com—a wondrously addictive reservoir of cheapskate, anticorporation knowledge and my freelance employer—I was shocked to read a post with lessons on how to avoid getting bumped from flights. My jaw dropped through the floor and my brain nearly exploded. How could such an oracular money-saving Web site give such counterintuitive advice? The post may as well have been a how-to guide to checking over your tax returns to make sure you're paying the IRS as much as possible.

There are few greater strokes of luck in this world than getting bumped off a flight. When the frazzled airline customer service lady hits her little "*piiiing*" public address button and informs you that the flight is overbooked and they're looking for people willing to take a later flight in return for a travel voucher, it's like a visit from the Tooth Fairy, Easter Bunny, Santa Claus, and Jessica Alba all rolled into one. Air travel is one of the most expensive and convenient ways to move about the country, and a free ticket is gold. Better than gold, even. Whenever given the choice between a ticket and a cash voucher, I always go with the ticket, punishing the airline by making sure I redeem the ticket voucher for a flight that's more expensive than the cash they were offering. With any luck, I'll be bumped off that flight as well and take another step toward my fantasy of never having to pay for another ticket in my life by getting continuously bumped and comped.

With that in mind, I resolve to twist the Consumerist's advice on itself, sprinkling in a little how-to knowledge of my own along with the inverse of the advice offered on the post.

- Show up late. All those post-9/11 warnings about needing to get to the airport three hours in advance are nonsense. The only purpose the warning serves is to clear out the way for people like me who prefer to cut it as close as possible and run down the terminal at the last second to catch my flight. I wouldn't recommend showing up as late as I do, but definitely avoid getting there hours in advance. Checking in sort of late-ish, meaning half an hour or so before the flight boards, means you won't be stuck in all the un-bumpable classes.

- Never check in through the Internet. Checking in online is the same thing as showing up for a flight infinity hours early. Those who want to get on the plane so badly are the last to make it onto that precious bump list.

- Pay less than full price for your ticket. Airlines, which foolishly think you don't want to get bumped, don't want to mess with customers dumb enough to pay full price for fares. They don't mind so much if lunatics such as you, who are always booking flights on Priceline and Orbitz and typing in discount codes while booking through the airline's site, go bother some other carrier. They think they're chasing you away by making you the most susceptible to a bump. Little do they know . . .

- Don't have many frequent-flier miles. All these programs are scams meant to inspire the gambling mentality in you that spurs you to take illogical leaps in order to make sure you're in the running for their half-assed "rewards," which carry ominous blackout dates and laughable restrictions. These plans inspire forced loyalty to airlines, causing you to swerve around better deals in order to stick with the company that gives you near-worthless miles. Another benefit of not signing up for these programs is that membership apparently makes you not so easily bumped. Okay, airlines, you've convinced me to forever fall out of love with your stingy frequent-flier bait-and-switches. You had me at "hell no."

All this applies to the forced bump. When you find yourself in a situation conducive to volunteer bumping, do your best to hold out and see if they sweeten up the deal a bit. Hover around the check-in desk, and if you see anyone make his way toward the desk after one of the offers, cut in front and take the deal before your opponent has the chance to snatch it away from you.

60. Dotcom Do-over

These relatively early days of the Internet are like the Wild West. Pioneers filled with dreams of riches are flooding the vast territory, staking their claims, and forging niches. As the potential of instant-flowing information and entertainment continues to develop, content providers are competing vigorously to round up as many loyal customers as possible, reasoning that one day their patrons will be so hooked that they'll be able to charge them for access.

Rival sites are engaging in arms races, investing more capital than they're taking in from ad revenue to win a virtual flexing contest. This is especially true of online news sources, including newspapers, whose owners blow insane budgets on salaries for writers, videographers, designers, and editors, as well as buyouts of competitors. It's all in the name of a mad rush to give away to as many nonpaying customers as possible the news they used to charge for, thus undercutting their subscriber base and hastening the medium's demise. In news publishers' board meetings, the online folks have to sell the idea that somewhere down the line they'll figure out how to get readers to pony up 50 cents a day to take a peek at the e-paper.

I'm convinced, however, that this fantasy in which customers pay for breaking news is just like flying cars and ginormous Voltron wars—things we hope for and imagine will be part of the future, but will never quite come. With each passing day, you and I only become more accustomed to getting everything online for free.

Some businesses out there are trying to jump the gun by making customers hand over money. This is as inane as 1955 Biff Tannen trying to become a millionaire by betting on sports without the benefit of the 2015 sports almanac given to him by time-traveling future Biff. All pay Web sites should be shunned until they no longer operate.

If you're paying for access to any site, cancel your subscription immediately because there are bound to be at least 100 others out there that will give you stuff that's at least as good for free. The only sites worth paying for are those that give you an embarrassment of essential material and occasionally ask for donations in return, such as Consumerist and Wikipedia. The key word here is "ask."

This truth holds for social networking, web hosting, sports, news, creative writing, and especially porn. A few examples to get you going: If you want the latest gaming information, avoid IGN's pay service in favor of Gamespot or Kotaku. If you're into the sports recruiting scene, avoid Rivals.com and run searches for the numerous hometown sports blogs run by insane fans who pull the info off sites such as Rivals and give it to you for free. If it's boobies you're after, ditch whatever credit-card-sapping pay site you're addicted to in favor of PersianKitty, which provides links to enough nudie pics to last you the rest of your perverted life.

The funny thing about offices is they're supposed to be places that help you earn money, yet they wind up being cesspools that suck away your income. Everyone always seems to be going around collecting money from people for some stupid reason. Some simple ground rules: Never join the lotto pool, buy anyone's Girl Scout cookies, sponsor fun runs, chip in to buy birthday cakes for people, or contribute to the coffee fund. Keeping your spare cash to yourself is at least as valuable as whatever mediocre raise your boss has planned.

61. Office Harvest

Just as no fast-food aficionado should ever need to purchase ketchup, no office worker should ever stoop to buying, *ahem*, let me gather my breath: pens, notepads, sticky notes, staples, Wite-Out, highlighters, pencils, or paper clips.

Did I cover everything there? Surely not, but feel free to fill in the blanks for whatever I might have left out. At the office, adhere to a mentality very much like the rule of thumb for hotel visits—take everything that isn't nailed down. Robbing your company's office supplies isn't so much thievery as it is an implied perk that you deserve for putting up with the ulcer-inducing nonsense you deal with every day.

You know you haven't done a good enough job swiping office supplies until you see a memo posted threatening employees with harsh punishment if they continue their evil ways. Just laugh off these declarations and don't let them affect the way you operate. It's management's job to figure out ways to stop you from scamming supplies by locking them down, which they will never do since they also steal blindly from the supply closet and need to keep access as open as possible so that when they're grilled by the higher-ups they can pass the blame for all the missing stuff onto their inferiors. It's a disjointed circle of life in which everyone has a part to play. The Discovery Channel should really do a documentary on the subject.

While I'll reemphasize that stealing office supplies should always be done, I'll add that the chicanery must be done with a measure of discretion. Never make it obvious, otherwise you'll only give your employer another reason to fire you. The best kleptomaniacs are those who operate like Sam Fisher from the *Splinter Cell* video games—move in the shadows and strike when an attack is least expected. A prime occasion for taking your pick of the workplace goods is early in the morning. Get to work before anyone else, pocket whatever you like—taking care to never open a new box or take a full container—then schlep it off to your car before anyone else gets there. The early-riser act serves a double purpose, making you appear to be a tenacious go-getter who can't wait to get his workday started and leaps out of bed in eagerness.

If the morning routine isn't your thing, you can be the night owl who stays until 10 PM, looking like the dedicated workaholic who can't peel himself away from his desk until the big project is finally completed, whereas in reality you're playing Tetris, simply waiting for the place to clear out so you can jam your coat pocket full of erasers. Staying late allows you to say goodbye to others in a condescending way, maybe while addressing a rival within earshot of the boss, "It must be nice to leave so early!" Of course, the inverse of the condescending goodbye is the condescending hello for those who come into work after you.

62. I Was Looking for a Pen

A nasty reality in all nonunion workplaces is pay scale inflation, which punishes seniority by placating veteran workers with bare-minimum raises and fellates fancy-pants newcomers with market-price salaries.

There's a reason the human resources department acts so discreetly when distributing paychecks and direct deposit stubs. It's not to protect your privacy but to exploit your ignorance. If you ever got a look at the salary figure of the guy two cubicles down, with five years' less experience than you and half your drive and talent, you'd go all Michael Douglas in *Falling Down* on the office space. Or maybe you'd just sulk in silence and whine about the inequity to your spouse. In any case, you wouldn't be a happy camper.

I've always believed in turning crap into crap-ade, however. A better response to discovering you're underpaid is to use it as justification for a raise you deserve. Bosses tend to be like bullies—let them push you around and they'll take your lunch money all your life. Stand up to them once and they may surprise you by giving in to your will. The best time to ask for a pay increase is, of course, your annual evaluation. Don't just walk in and demand more money; write up a boastful, highly exaggerated report of all the value you add to the office and include the thing about earning less than everyone around you. For extra credit, follow all that by lining up an outside job offer. It can come from a place you wouldn't actually ever want to work at or it can be fake altogether. Doesn't matter. Give your boss the assurance that you don't want to leave—you simply want to stay and be paid what you're worth, or at least earn what others with fewer qualifications and less talent are pulling in.

But how can you discover what the people around you are actually making? People guard the secret of what they make closer than the list of venereal diseases they've contracted throughout their lives. My instinct is to simply assume that you're getting paid the same or less than recent college graduates, because starting salaries tend to creep up at a slightly faster pace than whatever meager raises you've been netting in your years of service. If you'd like to bolster your claims with genuine facts, you'll need to do a little snooping. Be creative. Spontaneously run out of writing utensils, and muck around on others' desks. If you get caught, you were just looking to borrow a pen. Dig through the community trash on payday, hoping those with direct deposit will toss their stubs into the garbage.

Be on the alert for someone complaining that they left something in their car, then volunteer to go fetch it for them, saying you also left something in your ride. Take their keys and snoop through the crumpled papers in their backseat. A riskier option is to attempt to hack into your company's pay records or dig through HR files, but tread carefully here.

I've saved my personal favorite for last: Grab a copy of the staff directory and call ten phone numbers of those with similar positions, posing as a telemarketer and asking their yearly income. At least one of them is bound to cough up a salary figure.

Or, just avoid all the nonsense, be bold, and ask your colleagues what they make.

63. It Could Happen to Me

Company gift exchanges are the bane of my miserable existence. I see no purpose in buying random trinkets for people I'd never buy stuff for under normal circumstances in exchange for random trinkets bought by people who would never buy stuff for me under normal circumstances. I notice that some people experience genuine excitement when gathered round the table for the annual holiday present swap, and it helps me understand why the gift exchange exists. In a way I'm happy for these people that such a tedious custom can inject a tiny amount of joy into their mundane lives. It's just a shame that they feel they have to make me a part of it. And getting out of these things is harder than leaving the Hells Angels.

Every year around Thanksgiving, I make it a point to avoid all office meetings that may double as the occasion for passing the hat around and having everyone draw names. This only staves off the inevitable. Usually they'll draw for me and assign me a gifter and gift-ee. In my earlier years I've come out and asked not to be included, but doing so only got me scowls and contempt from the gift exchange mob. This would have been tolerable because I don't like those people anyway, but then one year the gift-exchange ringleader pinned me down in front of everyone and asked me if I'd participate in that year's event. I once called in sick the day of the exchange, hoping the whole thing would just blow over. The next day I found a useless Nerf basketball set with a bow on top waiting for me at my desk. I had to excuse myself and run off to Target to buy a baseball hat in order to make it look as though I hadn't forgotten.

Now I've given up on fighting gift exchanges and have whole-heartedly embraced the ceremony. Now my gift never changes—it's lottery tickets every year. It's a one-size-fits-all present that pops a little adrenaline into the proceedings, and the fact that it almost always results in no monetary gain for the receiver acts as my passive-aggressive jab at my forced participation in something I despise. Sometimes they'll win $10 or $20 and I'll look like a hero. Some people joke that I'll regret it when I give away a ticket that wins $100,000, that I'll wish I'd kept for myself, but they're wrong. Since I never play the lottery, I wouldn't feel entitled to the money on any tickets I bought as gifts. And I also reason, with possibly irrational hope, that if I ever did buy someone a jackpot, they'd be so grateful that they'd give me at least a little taste of the winnings. I'm thinking Nicolas Cage in *It Could Happen to You*, who plays a cop who gives half his winning lotto haul to a hot coffee shop waitress he felt bad for stiffing. I'm neither hot nor a waitress, but things could still work out for me.

Corporate Cataclysm

You can look at the relationship between consumers and corporations in two ways: one, that it's symbiotic and both parties need the other to survive in modern society, and two, that both sides are enemies looking to take maximum advantage of one another.

While recognizing that a world without corporations would fall apart, I reason that the corporate world is so strong that common folk are powerless to grind it to a halt. With that in mind, I think it's necessary to do everything you can to rip corporations off whenever possible because they're sure as heck ready to do the same to you. We may lack enough power to readily defend ourselves against corporate powers, but we do have the advantage of guerrilla fighters, striking in anonymity at sitting targets; Lilliputians slinging arrows against our giant, dumb enemies.

Herewith are my thoughts on messing with businesses for fun and profit.

64. How to Screw Over the McNopoly Game

Each year, McDonald's runs its Monopoly game, (which used to be called the "Best Chance Game") in which McDonald's value meals come with $1 Best Buy coupons. Best Buy dropped out of the promotion in the middle of the 00s decade, most likely because I worked the loopholes in the game so hard Best Buy could no longer afford pocket protectors for its Geek Squad. Toys R Us and Foot Locker stepped in in later years to fill the void, but two things about this "game" are givens: 1) McDonald's will always run this game with some sort of corporate partner, and 2) There will always be a way to use the game like a stretched-out tube sock.

For what it's worth, I'll describe exactly how I used to work the McNopoly game back when Best Buy was involved.

The following is a step-by-step program on how to violate this contest for all it's worth without having to eat any of McDonald's nasty food. This primer will teach you how I got a $40 video game with $22.50 of my own money. I understand that this feat isn't so impressive but recognize that my technique can be expanded exponentially. The more you take my advice, the more you'll be able to exploit this magical contest. For instance, you could multiply all these steps by seven, buy seven copies of a game, sell six on eBay, and make a hell of a profit. Without further ado:

Step one: Get ready to go. This journey will take you to a dollar store and a place that sells stamps. (You can also buy stamps online, but you'll have to wait a few days to get them.)

Step two: At the dollar store, buy fifty envelopes for $1.

Step three: Get fifty stamps. At 43 cents a pop, this will run you $21.50. Be sure to get sticker stamps, unless you want to do a ton of licking.

Step four: Do fifteen jumping jacks. You'll need to get the blood flowing for all the writing you're about to do.

Step five: Get your fifty envelopes out and affix a stamp in the upper right-hand corner of each.

Step six: Divide the stamped envelopes in two equal stacks. On the first stack, write your name and address on the bottom middle of the envelopes.

Step seven: Do twenty-five push-ups. Girl push-ups (using your knees to support you) are okay, but only if you're a girl.

Step eight: On the second stack, write your name and address on the upper-left corner of the envelopes.

Step nine: Do twelve deep knee bends to get the blood flowing once again. You're two-thirds of the way done!

Step ten: Visit the McDonald's contest Web site to find the mailing address, which is usually:

Monopoly 20XX Game at McDonald's

Game Piece Request

P.O. Box 49434

Strongsville, OH 44149

Step eleven: Fold each of the envelopes in stack one and stuff them one by one inside of corresponding envelopes in stack two. Seal them and mail them off.

Step twelve: Wait six to ten days for the envelopes to return with your game pieces. Do not eat at McDonald's during this time. But do go to McDonald's in order to pick up a free Monopoly game board. While you're there, search through the garbage cans (only the tops—don't dig through it, because that's nasty) for abandoned game pieces. Also search the countertops and look out for old people, who don't understand the contest and tend to leave game pieces behind as they go about their ways.

Step thirteen: Get your game pieces and lump together your Best Buy Bucks. You should have twenty-five Best Buy Bucks, at least two of which are of the $5 denomination, increasing your total amount of Best Buy money to $33.

Step fourteen: Open your other pieces. You should have enough to cover the entire board except for the winning pieces that don't actually exist. That's okay. Do not throw away your doubles, because you can use the codes on them for the online contest. You should also have two or three pieces that get you a free McDonald's value meal.

Step fifteen: Let's assume you have two free value meal pieces. Go to McDonald's again with one of your free value meal pieces and get a premium chicken sandwich meal. The sandwich box will come with a Best Buy Buck.

Step sixteen: Take the Best Buy Buck off the box, then take one bite of the sandwich. Chew a little then spit it out. Return it to the manager and say your sandwich doesn't taste right, which will be true because those things are nasty. The manager will give you another chicken sandwich. Take the Best Buy Buck off it, as well as any other game pieces that came with your meal, and throw it all away or give it to an unlucky homeless man.

Step seventeen: Repeat step sixteen later that night when a different manager is on duty. Doing this, searching in the trash, and random luck should leave you with $40 in Best Buy cash. If not, send out a couple more SASEs as needed.

Step eighteen: Log onto Playatmcd.com and enter ten codes per day. You should win lots of snap fish coupons and cell phone ring tones.

Step nineteen: Go to Best Buy and seize your prize from the stunned checkout clerk, who will be annoyed at being unlucky enough to have to serve the jerk who is buying a video game with $40 in Best Buy Bucks.

Step twenty: Raise your hands in victory!

65. Shut Me Up, Mr. Manager

An ounce of complaint is worth a pound of food. Restaurant managers are more paranoid than Kim Jong-Il, only instead of addressing threats with shoddy nuclear missile attacks, they'll send you coupons for free food in the mail.

Because there's so much competition among restaurants and so little to distinguish one place from another, a reputation for impeccable service and a policy of generous overcompensation for any shortcomings is all that keeps an eatery from having to shut down and sell the building to a Subway franchisee.

As a result, diners have become finicky freak-jobs who whine like babies over the tiniest, most inconsequential details. Rare is the restaurant higher-up who doesn't roll over and give the customer everything he or she wants, which only encourages more of a complaining culture. In effect, we eaters are the surly, overgrown bullies who have been left back a grade and the restaurant management is the nerd who we get to do our homework and give up their milk money.

The way to take advantage of the social norm is to blend in and complain even on restaurant visits that go smoothly. When it comes to food, there is always something wrong, and even if there isn't, you can always make something up.

I discovered this modus operandi one time after coming down with food poisoning at a stuffed burrito-making fast-food chain. A stale tortilla had me sidelined for forty-eight hours, and once I recovered I made an angry call to the number on my receipt. A day later the money I paid for the meal was refunded to my credit card and two certificates for free meals were in my mailbox. Then it occurred to me—why wait until my next food poisoning to get a free meal and gift certificates?

I immediately grabbed a phone book, flipped it to the restaurants section, and dialed up every place I liked and filed a complaint. I told each manager I had eaten there Saturday night and walked away devastated by my experience. I improvised the circumstances of each as I went. For some, I griped that the service was bad, always refusing to provide a name or description of the person who served me in order to keep from someone getting fired. For others, I said the food was undercooked, and I didn't send it back because it took so long for me to get the meal in the first place and I was in a hurry to get on with my evening. Sometimes I insisted the music was too loud or the dishes weren't clean. To a man, everyone I talked to offered a free meal to smooth things over. About half of them did what I was hoping for, taking down my address to send me a coupon. The others asked to see me personally on my next visit so they could "take care of me," which I politely declined and insisted I was only giving them the information to help improve their business, all the while silently seething that they weren't giving me what I wanted. I would never walk into a restaurant identifying myself as a complainer, because that would be just begging to get spit or snot in my meal.

I could tell quite a few of the people I talked to didn't quite believe what I was telling them, but they gritted their teeth nevertheless to make me happy. To these folks I responded, "I don't like your tone, sir!" and threatened to hang up, which set them straight. The customer may not always be right, but he'll get his way if he's a big enough dick about it.

66. Problem Management

D ante had it easy. He had to endure only nine circles of hell, whereas anyone who confronts corporate voice mail must traverse far more layers of phone-wrought damnation.

I'm convinced it's a common business practice, particularly with medical offices, phone companies, and banks, to levy random, unwarranted charges against you, hoping you look over the fact that you don't owe what the invoice says and pay it blindly. As another backup, businesses put endlessly cycling, user-antagonistic systems in place. These loops are meant to prevent you from reaching a live human, draining your will to complain, and simply pay the charges in order to avoid a black mark on your credit report.

In the earlier days of the voice mail netherworld, you could bypass most of the nonsense by tapping the single-finger salute known as the "0" key, which patched you through to an operator. Nowadays, voice mail service designers have gotten a bit more crafty and have changed the operator hotkey to another number or taken it out altogether. Of course, once you reach a human, you may wish you hadn't.

These people are the worst kind of mean, which is outright cruelty masquerading in politeness. Customer service operators are paid to not let you get your way. And yet they are powerless to deny your request to kick it up to the next level of management. In fact, it's usually the act of asking to speak to a higher-up that leads the asshole you're dealing with to settle your dispute.

A few vocabulary words to use interchangeably as small threats: "supervisor," "unacceptable," "media," and "Better Business Bureau."

Ah yes, the BBB, my Best Beat-down Buddy. The mere mention of the three letters is like what happens in the cartoons when a victim mentions the name "Batman" to a jewel thief. I've filed many a complaint simply so I could use it as a bargaining chip when negotiating my way out of mistreatment. One time an auto shop charged me $800 for a repair that should have been covered under warranty, and thanks to my offer to rescind my BBB complaint, I got a full refund.

It's rare that you have to step it up to the BBB level to get the problem resolved. Usually you just have to talk to a goober, who passes you onto another goober or two until you find someone with the ability and willingness to help you.

Whenever you're told, "I don't have the power to cancel that fee," that's when you ask to step up to the next level. It usually happens that the supervisor is on vacation the week you're complaining, which is probably just another crafty trick to make you forget about the whole thing.

Once you finally get a hold of someone who does have the authority to give you what you're after, but simply denies you cold, you'll need to ask for his boss, whether or not he's part of the customer service department. I love it when the customer service heads refuse to send me on to the higher-ups by insisting it's their call on whether or not to help me with my problem.

"Oh really, you're the owner of the company are you?" I say. "Congratulations!" The sarcasm will either get me a referral to the corporate headquarters or, if I'm lucky, hung up on, giving me more ammunition to use when I do talk to corporate.

I have never lost a battle on something falsely charged to me because I never give in, and I find no amount of money too small to fight for. Climb the ladder high enough, and you'll eventually find someone who's so self-important they can't be bothered by your insignificant gripe, so they'll let you get your way.

67. Buy Low, Sell High

Get-rich-quick schemes rarely work. It's the get-rich-slowly plans that pay dividends.

One of my favorites involves signing up for introductory offers at DVD clearinghouses such as Columbia House, which cut you good deals if you buy twelve or so films, then turning around and selling them online.

It works like this: They bait you in with a tantalizing opening deal, offering five DVDs for free* or nine for the price of one.* The asterisks, of course, are the tricky parts, signifying in tiny type that you'll have to pay shipping and handling for all your DVDs, including the supposedly free ones, and that you're required to buy a certain number of films at full price within a set time limit afterward, otherwise you'll be in violation of the agreement, which can lead to collections and dings on your credit rating.

I know some people who have managed to weasel out of the contracts by simply ignoring the harassing phone calls, e-mails, and mailings demanding that they pay up, but I don't like to mess with that kind of thing. I'll buy my required full "club price" DVDs along with my first order, just so I can be done with it, quit, and then be able to take advantage of the intro offer again as soon as possible.

Sticking with the club is the wrong way to go because things are never quite as sweet afterward, and the "special club price" of the featured monthly films is usually more expensive than those of electronics warehouses.

Before you sign up, be sure to actually read through the user agreements before clicking like a madman to finish out your order. These plans are run by shifty types who are always changing up the agreements, including the amount of movies you're required to buy at full price after you've received your "free" films. Then scan through the online reseller you plan on using and take note of the DVDs that are drawing the highest minimum prices so you know what to order. It's often the best idea to order movies of a particular series or genre and sell them in a lot—that way you can up your profit margin by cutting down on shipping costs. It's also less of a hassle than having to trek to the shipping place each time a customer orders one of your movies.

I've only done the DVD thing a couple times and I've ended up keeping most of the ones I ordered because I'm insane about wanting to own every movie I love, and these clubs help me fill out my collections for cheaper than it would take to order them individually. But I have a friend who's hard-core into this scheme and he ratchets up my ideas a few notches, tossing in some low-risk mail fraud with it. He orders large packages of DVDs to addresses of vacant houses, then drives by on delivery day to pick them up and resell them. Sometimes he'll call the company and complain that the DVDs never arrived and get an entirely new identical shipment sent out before he finally pays up. Exposure to such frauds is the price these companies pay when they're too cheap to spring for delivery confirmation service.

68. Return Policy Guide

It would be foolish to print a comprehensive guide to retailers' return policies, which fluctuate with a frequency akin to the stock market—Consumerist.com is a gold mine for keeping you updated on the latest adjustments, which are usually made in the direction of added stinginess—but I can give you some always-applicable guidelines that should help you become the best returner you can be of unwanted gifts, defective items, and clothing you only needed for one night.

I find returning much more fulfilling than buying. It feels like you're making the business yield to you, buying back junk that has little value to you for full retail price. This is especially true of awful presents without gift receipts that you pawn off for store credit. My advice here will do the most for that most diffi-cult of returns, the receipt-less take-back. If you've got a receipt, the process will be easy for you unless you break the time limit that's probably printed right there. Without paper evidence of your purchase, you're working without a net, and for good reason.

Without a receipt, the store can't verify that they actually sold the item, although most can track purchases if you give them a credit-card number. In drafting its return policy, compa-nies have to straddle a precarious line between appearing accom-modating and sketchy; protecting itself from return fraud while not coming off as a street hustler who ducks into the nearest alley after he sells you a fake Rolex from inside his overcoat. These days it's a general rule that if you've got something unopened or in pristine condition worth less than $20, you can return it without much of a problem for store credit. Cash back for receipt-less returns nowadays is more difficult than coaching the Detroit Lions to a Super Bowl title and take a Jedi-like influence over a customer service manager that I lack. So bear in mind that if you don't bring little slips of paper proving your purchase to the return desk, you won't be walking away with green paper imprinted with dead presidents.

Things you'll never be allowed to return are software and electronics, unless you claim they're defective. To save yourself some grief, don't peel off the plastic until you're sure you want to watch the film, upload the program, or play the game. Likewise with food—if you've opened it, you're keeping it forever unless it's rotten or stale, in which case you can usually work out an exchange.

With everything else, it's a fat, blurry line that wavers depending on minute details as well as the mood of those involved with the transaction. Courtesy and, if applicable, flirtation will go a long way toward success here. Be patient and kind, and don't vary your story of how you came into the item because you'll have to undergo a mini cross-examination by the customer service clerk as well as the manager she'll call over to approve the return by sticking his key into the cash register. Treat it like a police questioning—say as little as possible because yammering on is a sign of nerves and insecurity.

As far as the item you're bringing back, make sure it's free of dirt or signs of use, and if it's clothing, bring it back unwashed and folded in the exact style of the store. For packaged things, bring back the full box, as well as all the foam and plastic packaging within, as well as all accessories. Many a TV return has been scuttled because of a lack of a remote. Make sure whatever you're bringing back looks so good it can easily be placed back on the rack and blend right in with the rest of the merchandise. On the other hand, if you can't get something back into perfect condition, don't rule yourself out by not chancing a return. Just like the lottery, you can't win if you don't play.

Some final notes: Always pause at the entrance to let the greeter tab a little dated sticker on your return item, lest you get to the return counter and have them think you just pulled the thing off the shelves. And strive to make your returns visits on evenings and weekends—the busier they are, the better it is for you because they won't want to take the extra time to analyze your bring-back.

69. Unwarranted Advances

Despite the way it's taken more money from my paychecks than social security, I've always loved me some blackjack. For those who don't know, it's the simple casino table game in which you're initially dealt two cards, then must take as many as you need to get to twenty-one points without going over. The game of blackjack can teach you much about life: Everyone else around you always seems to have better luck than you. The only thing more disgusting than smoking is breathing in secondhand smoke. Gambling is evil and drunken gambling is as dangerous as drunken driving.

But the most important lesson blackjack can teach you is to never, ever get insurance. Whenever a dealer shows an ace, he asks if anyone at the table wants to order insurance, which means hedging your bet in a side wager that cuts your losses in half if it turns out the dealer has an unbeatable blackjack.

The thing is no one ever takes insurance because doing so is not only a wuss move, it's also plain stupid. The odds say a dealer with an ace showing has less than a 30 percent chance of hitting a blackjack, so insurance is a sucker bet meant to play on your insecurities. If you're playing at a table with anyone who knows what they're doing, a signal for insurance makes you look like not only a fool but also a wimp. Still, like other idiotic things such as bungee jumping or skydiving, taking blackjack insurance is something for everyone to try just once, if only to take in the shock that discourages you from ever doing it again. Take insurance at the table and you'll look around and see a lot of head-shaking and condescending glances. Keep those looks in mind whenever you're out in the real world and a salesman offers you insurance, extended warranties, stain sealant on furniture, or rust protection on a car.

The only insurances I approve of getting are car and home because they're required by law and health because our Darwinian style of healthcare will charge you approximately $1.2 million to heal a broken arm if you don't have insurance.

Salesmen are smart about the way they hit you with insurance. They wait until you've committed to your purchase, having listened to them gush in saccharine sweet talk about the virtues of whatever product they've coaxed you into buying. Then just before you're ready to seal the deal and walk away, they start playing on your insecurities, hinting that if something should go wrong with the piece of perfection they just sold you, you're out of luck unless you pony up an extra 5 percent to buy the super-duper, special, enhanced-warranty protection program. Don't fall for it. They push so hard not because they care about whatever they're selling you, but because they're aiming to eke out an extra commission on top of what they've already got coming. They're treating you like a baby, trying to get you to nuzzle up against a teddy bear–printed blanky you can use to get your ignorant little head to sleep at night.

You'll have to turn away hard-selling mini-speeches, including horror stories of customers who have had problems in the past or the old "I wouldn't let my own child walk out of here without this coverage" line, to which you can reply, "Yeah, but I bet your children wouldn't have to pay for it."

While you're turning down the pleas, keep in mind that you've scratched up and dented everything you've ever bought in your past, you're happy enough with all of it, and this thing will be no different. Also, if there's a manufacturing problem with your new purchase, you can always hit up the implied warranty or return it, getting your little teddy bear blanky peace of mind for free.

Gross, Mean, and Just Plain Wrong—and Yet Oh So Profitable

Forgive me, Father, for what I'm about to write. I'm not even Catholic and I feel as though I have to confess—that's just how dirty, underhanded, and straight-up cruel the advice I'm about to dole out to you is. Let me make clear that the advice from here on out is strictly for laughs, and I'm not held responsible if you actually enact any of this insanity.

Try any of these heinous tactics and you'll be in need of a soul cleansing, but you'll also have a bigger bank account and great stories to tell at parties.

70. No Aspeaka

I take the title for this chapter from a line in the comedy *Black Sheep*, in which a ruthless politician uses the term to describe the English-speaking ability of her illegal immigrant maid. Learning to say the words "No aspeaka" in particular situations is the key to hacking hundreds off your yearly expenses and possibly thousands if you're unfortunate enough to suffer a major medical emergency.

Just remember to forget how to speak English and you'll never have to pay for an emergency room visit, and thus have no real need for health insurance.

Our nation's healthcare system tends to get a bad rap, but it's really quite excellent, depending on your perspective. For the ultrarich, the healthcare system is wonderful because the finest medicine and health practitioners flock to the United States, meaning the best care is always immediately available so long as price isn't an object. The system works even better for illegal immigrants, whom hospitals won't turn away even if they're uninsured and lack the means to pay for the care. The U.S. health-system naysayers come from the end of the spectrum of middle and lower class citizens, who know English, are citizens, and thus need to fork over a ludicrous percentage of their bankroll in order to make sure they don't die of pneumonia, they're immune from fatal diseases, and their limbs don't fall off.

Chances are you come from this tragic subset of society, so the onus is on you to move into one of the more favored categories. Joining the ultrarich isn't really an option, so basically society is forcing you to pretend you're an illegal immigrant in order not to get gouged to get what ails you fixed.

If you ever feel a heart attack coming on, immediately race off to an emergency room and make sure to take your cell phone, wallet, and any other identifying paraphernalia off your person immediately. Then either drive to a hospital and crawl your way to the emergency entrance or pound on the door of someone in the neighborhood who doesn't recognize you and immediately start screaming in gibberish. If you have time, you can also sell your foreign-ness up a bit by dressing a part. Keep a kit of tattered, foreign-looking clothes in your closet, your car, and in your desk at work for such an occasion.

Whenever someone says anything to you, scream your lungs out in the manner you think a foreigner might, for instance adding in yelps at odd times and cursing bizarrely named gods. If you happen to know a foreign language, then fall back on that and tell whatever interpreter bill collector the hospital sics on you some story about how you're visiting here from out of the country, but you can go through with the effort even if you used to fall asleep in junior high Spanish class.

Allow yourself to pass out whenever possible, and scrawl odd, made-up characters onto whatever forms assistants shove in front of your face. Communicate mostly in gestures, pointing to the area of your body that's affecting you. Try not to speak clearly, and when pressed, fall back on the phrase, "No aspeaka." Saying the words can make you sound vaguely Latino, African, Eastern European, or Asian, depending on whatever your appearance and skin tone demands. Make yourself a loud nuisance and the hospital staff will be more loathe to ask you questions and quicker to treat you and get you out the door. It's possible you may be turned over to the police, but a well-timed scamper before you've checked out of the hospital will save you the trouble.

71. Pound Your Dog

As costly as it is to pay for your own medical mishaps, it's even more expensive, and less reasonable, to pay when your dog falls deathly ill or is injured. It doesn't make fiscal sense to fix up your puppy because the price of having him put to sleep and then adopting a replacement pooch is almost always miniscule as compared to having him professionally nursed back to health, but you want to do right by your doggie because you love him so darn much.

So that's why you have to follow the old maxim: If you truly love a creature who happens to be mortally wounded, abandon him outside a progressive, no-kill pound or pet rescue facility, then swoop in and adopt him once he's all healed up.

This world is filled with kind, lonely folk who—brutally disappointed in their human interactions—turn to the automatic love of animals as a weak substitute to fill the gaping maw inside their pathetic hearts.

These people are in love with the innocence and helplessness of pets and thus divert all their resources to saving as many as possible. You can either be annoyed with the naiveté of these types or accept that it takes all kinds to make a world and abuse the sentiment to your betterment.

You do risk the ownership of your animal if you go this route, because someone else might adopt him before you're able to get him back, but comfort yourself in the knowledge that whoever takes your pup will almost certainly be a kind and caring owner—one who'd never resort to creepy, exploitative shenanigans in order to save a buck when the pet gets sick again. Odds are, however, you and Fido will be back together after he's been taken care of. No-kills and rescue societies are adamantly particular about who they'll let take in their little angels, so make sure your house looks to be in good, pet-caring shape and make sure to hide your backyard bulldog fighting ring.

When abandoning your pet, make sure to wear a disguise as you carry him into the joint, then drop him off without a word, providing any particulars about the injury or condition of the dog with a note attached to his collar—ID tag removed, of course. Wait two weeks and then stroll into the facility with a specific description of what sort of dog you're looking for. You'll make

some eighteen-year-old intern's eyes light up when you say you're in the market for a brown lab mix who's at least a few years old. What do you know, out will trot your old friend. He'll be happy to see you since dogs are dumb and don't care when you've risked losing them in their darkest hour, and the folks who run the clinic will be overjoyed to see the way the old boy has taken to you. They'll be convinced they've found a soul mate and that their tireless efforts are responsible. Little will they know they've reduced themselves to pawns at your bidding.

72. Rags to 'Wiches

Who says soup kitchens are only for the homeless?

Every night, especially in the dead of winter, there's a bounty of free, delicious food available without a catch. All you need to do is line up patiently, plate in hand, and wait for the goods. As you'd expect in such a situation, the clientele isn't exactly the ritziest, but hanging with a rough crowd is a small consolation to score free eats.

I caught on to this phenomenon one day a few years ago at work, when I grabbed a bagel off the break desk.

"Don't touch those," a do-gooder coworker squawked once my hand was in the figurative cookie jar. "They're for the shelter."

As I ate the bagel anyway, I apologized and asked what I could do to help. She suggested I bring a few loaves of bread and help with her weekly volunteer gig serving the homeless. I, of course, declined, because I had important plans to play *Metroid Prime 2: Echoes* that night, but the germ of the idea had begun to grow.

The great thing about faking homelessness is that everyone pretty much takes you at face value. They don't hand out ID cards to verify you've been thrown out of your apartment and fired from your job and now spend all your days begging for pennies you save up for booze. All you need to do is dress down a bit, avoid shaving for a few days, and forget to comb your hair. I can't speak for you, but it's much easier for me to pass as a homeless person than as a contributing and upstanding member of society.

Once you've taken in a few free homeless meals you'll see why it is that people remain homeless. It's not so bad, and the food is as good or better than junior high cafeteria fare. Sometimes it's much better, even. In many cases, high-profile chefs with TV news cameras in tow donate their time to soup kitchens, meaning that when you're stuffing your face full of grub on camera for a feel-good story, most people sitting at home watching you will be eating far less glamorously, and thus will be jealous of your meal. Homeless folks are largely a jovial lot, filled with stories from the road and wry societal observations. There are, of course, a few angry crazies, but surely the same is true at your office.

If you're feeling enterprising, you may as well take your car out, park a couple blocks away from the shelter—you don't want anyone to see you getting out of your car, plus there's a good chance people will randomly hand you money when you're walking down the street looking homeless—then take your food to go and hit up the next shelter, and then the next. If you live in an adequately large city you can collect an entire week's worth of dinners with just one night's work.

73. Wet Bar

Ever get drunk at a bar, open a tab, and spend way too much money buying yourself and others drinks? A quick, easy, and no-cost way out of it is to wait until the bar is at its busiest, which will most likely be last call when there's a mad rush to close out all the credit-card tabs before everyone is shoved out the door and left to fend for themselves against the waiting army of drunk tank cops.

Ask for your credit-card receipt, say for $300, then stare at it in a slow daze until the barkeep gives up on you and saunters away to take care of someone else. Then you sloppily sign it in a signature that doesn't look much like yours and rest it in the sloppiest pile of condensation on the bar you can find. Make sure to have the receipt soak up the water very well so that as much of the signature as possible is destroyed. As soon as your receipt is suitably sopped up, get out of there before the barkeep can get back to check on you.

A couple weeks later when the charge has reached your account and the statement is about to come out, call the credit-card company and claim the bill was supposed to be $30 instead of $300. They may tell you to work it out with the bar, but be a little stubborn—maybe think about tossing off a threat or two to cancel your card due to shoddy customer service—and you can get them to take care of it for you. Most of the time it will end in your favor right there. Businesses don't like to take stands against credit-card companies, which can pull their services and leave the bar unable to take the majority of their customers' payments.

For the bar to make a solid case in contesting the dispute with your credit-card peeps, they'll need to produce a legible receipt, which thanks to your shenanigans they won't be able to do. The bar owner may call you up at that point to bicker, and may even ask to meet you in person, but always refuse and tell him you'd rather take the issue to small-claims court. In all likelihood he'll just let the difference of $270 go without any further fight. You've just saved yourself some cash, you drunken moron.

74. Bar-Keep

The trendier, busier, and more upscale the bar, the more likely the staff is willing to let big tips sit on the counter for minutes on end. I've never tended bar, so I can't claim to understand the psychology of what it takes to let good money sit all perky and vulnerable-like for extended periods of time. I theorize maybe these guys don't mind letting big bills dangle for a while in hopes they will serve as rumpled green billboards coaxing others to tip as generously. Or maybe they're self-conscious, worried that whoever left the cash is lurking back in the crowd, waiting for change, and the barkeep would prefer to bide his time in order to avoid the tragic indignity of having to shoot out the pathetic bellboy look. You know, the one that says, "Do you need change, sir? Or may I pocket your humble crumbs as I scamper back to my loser-cave?"

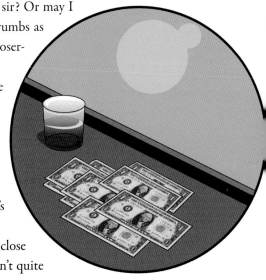

You can see where I'm going with this, I'm sure. To do a Bar-Keep, you eye a lonely, abandoned $20, wait for just the right moment when nobody's looking, and pocket it.

The technique is close to thievery, but it doesn't quite

cross the boundary that say, nabbing a tip off a restaurant table would. Because the money's sitting on a public space, it's highly feasible to spectators that any person bold enough to pick up money resting on the bar is the one who either put it down or has it coming to him. Confidence and a bored look in your eyes are keys here. Ninja-like quickness doesn't hurt a bit either.

The Bar-Keep is highly risky and liable to get you permanently 86ed from an establishment or, worse, taken in the backroom and beaten within inches of your life by beefy bouncers. The reward for pulling it off is scant, $20 maximum, and comes with a lifelong chaser of regret and shame. Your friends, though, will hold you in as high regard as Han Solo—a daring adventurer who risks life and limb in order to show he's the stealthiest Millennium Falcon pilot in the galaxy.

I've never turned this trick myself, nor would I, for the Bar-Keep is probably the only play in this book so cruel that it's even below my scandalous depths. I have seen it done once, in Vegas, by a wildly drunken friend who was out of gambling money and promptly lost the heisted bar tip on one hand of blackjack. I think my friend was a moron, but I don't exactly cry myself to sleep for the bartender who missed out on his $20. My message for the hordes of barkeeps who will surely send me hate mail for including this section: If there's money on the bar, take it, you jackasses. Or my drunken, gambling addict friend will.

75. There's Mischief in My Pizza

Real simple: Order a pizza with three or four toppings, then call and complain once it's delivered, claiming the cook screwed up on your order. You demand they send over the correct pizza for free quickly, lest you switch your eternal allegiance to Papa John's (Pizza Hut managers are the most susceptible to Papa John's threats because, unless Wikipedia tells me wrong, the two companies are rivals whose history goes way back).

After the manager quadruple checks your new order, they'll send another delivery guy with a new pie. Once he gets there, company protocol may dictate that he asks for the old pizza back, giving you a couple of options before he gets to your house: Either snarf a couple pieces of the supposedly screwed-up pizza and hand him back the remains or get greedy and keep the whole thing, insisting you threw it away out of disgust. The plan is foolproof, thanks to the inherent power of the consumer. You may occasionally run into a jaded, smartass manager who brushes off your contention that you ordered pepperoni and mushroom, not pepperoni, mushroom, and olive, by simply telling you to pick off the olives. Your standard reply: "I'm allergic to olive oil—you wanna pay for an emergency room visit?"

There's also a possibility of confronting a snobbish manager who's onto your scheme and is bent on proving, even if he has to resort to courtroom tactics, that he took your order down correctly. This guy tries to act like whatever it says on his little computer screen must be right: "Well, it says you ordered olives!"

The way to deal with this situation is to come right back at him with circumstantial evidence. Calmly state, "Well obviously you thought I ordered olives, otherwise it wouldn't have been typed into your program and the olives wouldn't have shown up on my pizza. But I never said olives. Maybe I said, 'That's all' and it was garbled over the phone."

The customer is always right, even when he's wrong. Consider this from the perspective of a manager. When a client calls and claims his order was taken down incorrectly, you have two choices: A) Believe the crater-faced sixteen-year-old you've got working the phones and risk alienating a customer and all his family and friends, or B) Send over a pizza that costs you a couple bucks to make and be done with it. Hell, you've even had pizzas delivered from your place to your own house and had the orders turn out wrong. Give the guy his damn pizza and maybe red-flag his phone number in case he tries to pull this malarkey the next time. Let him pull the same scam on the 8,000 other pizza places in town, but never again on you, he reasons.

Shut up and give me my free pizza, beyotch, you mentally counter.

76. Making DVD Scratches Disappear

A h, Netflix, how do I love thee? Let me count the ways:
You let me watch hours of *Entourage* and *Sopranos* on-end without having to spring for the boxed sets.

You give me astute suggestions of movies and TV series I'll enjoy without me having to do any research myself.

You presto-change-o my scratched-up DVDs—which got that way because I unwisely lent them out to heathen friends— into fresh, immaculate discs so shiny I can look deep into the silicone and see my sunken, caved-in eyes.

And sometimes you even add bonus features that came out with newer, extra special-er editions of my movies.

By ordering movies you already own and pulling the old switcheroo, you can partake in the truly full benefits of a Netflix membership. Sure, it's morally wrong to do so and probably runs counter to one of the user agreements you check off on when you're applying for your membership, but whatevs. Netflix deserves the treatment because they screw you over plenty often, sending you scratched-up, unplayable discs on countless occasions. In one instance I received a copy of *Valley Girl* that was snapped completely in half. The jagged edges could have poked my eye out, but I took the mishap like a man. When you pseudo-accidentally mail the company back the wrong DVD, all you're doing is returning the favor. Angry that your 2002 DVD of *Casablanca* was rendered obsolete by the 2004 edition? Do the switcheroo. Your copy of *Basic Instinct* always skips in chapter 17? Switcheroo! *The Departed* disc you lent to grandma is plagued with coffee stains in a pattern that matches her end table doily? Can I get a SWITCH. Can I get an A. Can I get a ROO.

Aw, shut up Netflix corporate honchos who are shaking your fists in anger. Your genius business model nets you more bank than Michael Jordan's ex-wife and you know you budget to lose a certain amount of DVDs a year not only to scratches but also to outright theft and mail fraud at the hands of people like my profiteering pal Jackson, who is far more ruthless than me. Relax and upgrade my regular *There's Something About Mary* to the unrated *There's Something More About Mary*. And act like you like it.

77. Tipping IS Just a City in China

"I don't tip because society says I have to. All right, if someone deserves a tip, if they really put forth an effort, I'll give them something, a little something extra. But this tipping automatically, it's for the birds. As far as I'm concerned, they're just doing their job."
—Mr. Pink (Steve Buscemi) in Reservoir Dogs

I refer you to the Quentin Tarantino masterpiece because everything Mr. Pink says in the film's diner scene is resoundingly true. In addition to the above diatribe, Pink makes some astute points:

- If waiters don't make enough money in their jobs, they can quit.
- Waiters' jobs aren't any more difficult than those of fast food, and yet society doesn't deem you should tip them.
- It doesn't matter that waiters are taxed on expected tips, because by tipping you're playing into the demented game. Better, and cheaper, to show your support for the unfair plight to which the government has exposed waiters by signing a petition in favor of repealing the law.

To Mr. Pink's philosophy I'd add that tipping is a tiresome practice bound by arcane rules that's best avoided whenever possible. The whole 15 percent of the post-tax check figure rule of thumb—why does a waiter deserve more money for bringing me a steak instead of a salad?—is as asinine as mechanics' notion that cars need their oil changed every 3,000 miles. Car manuals clearly state that oil changes every 5,000 miles will do you just fine, and since restaurants don't come with manuals, I'll write a universal one right here and now, and it will only take two words: Don't tip.

By the way, if you're ever on a date with a hot waitress or ex-waitress, this rule goes into the shredder faster than Kenneth Lay's sensitive Enron documents. Tip and tip big, and whenever you're in a conversation about tipping philosophy with a hot current or ex-waitress, make up some cock-and-bull story about how they deserve it and how you feel so bad for waitstaff for how little they're paid. My favorite line for this purpose: "Sure, they say the guidelines for tipping are 15 to 18 percent, but I usually don't go below 25 percent. Those people just work so darn hard!" It's a lie that will get you laid.

Tips for hot waitresses aren't tips at all but investments in preferred stock that potentially pay off in dividends of poonanny.

Other exceptions include days in which your car's cup holder is overflowing with pennies and dimes. There's no better way to get rid of change than to dump it on a Denny's table after munching down your Grand Slam as a heartfelt thank you to the ever-phenomenal service. Also, tip regularly at places you're a regular—you never want to be served by a waiter who remembers you didn't tip him the last time—and of course tip really hot women. The tip you leave, if any, should always directly correlate to how badly you want to have sex with the person serving you.

78. Long-term Rental with Benefits

Always be on the lookout to exploit moronic loyalty programs that let you build up store credit by making purchases. Such incentives are basically handwritten notes begging you to legally steal stuff off the store shelves. Two of my favorites are at Suncoast and Best Buy. Both stores offer rewards clubs that track your purchases, which give you points that accrue into gift cards worth a tiny percentage of what you've spent. The key is to rack up the free store credit without actually handing over your dough.

Here's what you do: Sign up for a membership, make a colossal purchase on a credit card with a decent grace period (forty-five days or so) in order to avoid ever having to actually pay for the items, wait until the requisite points are credited to your account, cash them in as gift certificates, and then return the stuff you bought.

A few years ago I used the method to raid the Suncoast shelves for $300 worth of merchandise. I made sure to pick up DVD sets I could sell on the side if something with my plan fell through—*Sopranos*, the original *Star Wars* trilogy, and the like. I was armed with a double-points coupon meant to draw new members, and I ended up with certificates for $60 in free DVDs mailed to me. Sure, I looked like an ass returning a bag full of DVDs, but it was well worth the embarrassment to check my credit-card account a couple days later to see my balance wiped clean. And it felt even better to walk into the same store the next day and cash in my disloyalty rewards.

A couple guidelines: Study the fine print on the club's rules before making your move, and be sure you're making a killing that will stick and turn into instant bonuses. Mind the minimums and limits. You neither want to go too small and risk not getting anything for your efforts, nor do you want to max out your credit card for diminished returns.

Corporations have taken steps toward locking these babies down by not crediting your account with points until at least thirty days after the purchase, but you can tiptoe around the barrier by asking for a gift receipt—which typically employs return periods far longer than regular purchases—whenever you buy your stuff. Be vigilant on scouting for special bonus points promotions, and whenever you hear someone's in the market for something from one of your club-membership stores, such as, say, an ink cartridge from Best Buy, volunteer to pick it up for them in exchange for reimbursement. If you've got any shut-in pals who love to order stuff online, you can form a symbiotic relationship. You save them on the wait time and shipping fees while they fatten up your points balance.

79. This Space for Rent

Bless video-game companies for launching their new consoles with overactive hype machines, then following up the mania with weak production. The phenomenon produces lines outside electronics and games stores that resemble Moscow breadlines during the Soviet era. The queues consist almost entirely of fanboys and enterprising eBay hucksters pining for vouchers that will let them purchase their precious systems once the store opens. I've got another name for these line-dwellers: suckers. Only idiots wait in line for twelve hours for a system they'll be able to pick up without a wait in only a couple months' time, and only the daring brave the lines only for the right to risk the wild wilderness of online resale for a dubious return.

The smartest way to handle such situations of mass hysteria is to visit the lines with the intention of selling your spot to stragglers who dodder into the party hours late. Wear a placard that says, "This space for sale" and you can quickly find yourself in a bidding war for your spot. A buddy of mine got $300 for my upfront perch in a PlayStation 3 line in late 2006—he gladly

handed it over for his two hours' work. Sure, he might have been able to flip the console on eBay for a couple thousand at the time but that would have required at least ten more hours of waiting, which he simply wasn't into. Had he been more enterprising, he might have been able to take half of that $300 and buy a spot a few clicks back, then resell it at an even greater profit once a pathetic, eager-to-please weekend dad strolled along with a nagging 10-year-old at his side. He took the money and ran, and I did the same in April of '07 when I nabbed $30 for giving up my spot after fifteen minutes outside a Best Buy for a Wii. Some clueless dad gingerly handed me over three $10 bills, feeling as though he was being taken advantage of. "I guess I can just say I paid you to wait in line for me!" he said with a fake chuckle as he dropped the money into my hand. You sure did, chump.

Console releases may be usually few and far between, but you can also employ the strategy at lines for professional teams' playoff games, cult favorite restaurant openings such as In-N-Out Burger, and even outside department or toy stores on Black Fridays, especially when the media has whipped the public into idiotic frenzies about holiday gifts in short supply, such as the Tickle Me Elmo. Make 'em tickle you with a Hamilton if they want Santa to deliver on his promise to their rugrat.

80. Defective is Defective

Video-game and DVD retailers stick it to you by refusing to accept opened disc packages for returns. Should you accidentally buy a copy of *Pootie Tang*, *Kangaroo Jack*, or *Kung Pow! Enter the Fist* and not realize the error of your ways until you've broken the seal, the policy leaves you with little recourse other than lugging it over to a used DVD shop, where you'll quite possibly be put through the indignity of fingerprinting and a driver's license check for a measly 50 cents in cash or a dollar in store credit. Sure, you could march the DVD back to the store and appeal to a manager, but ninety-nine times out of 100 you'll only be wasting your breath. After all, it says right there on the receipt that the company doesn't accept opened DVDs or software for returns. The manager can just tell you to read the receipt, making you look like an ass in front of everyone behind you in line.

Notice a few sentences ago, however, that I said "little recourse," not "no recourse." There's a devious, deceptively obvious magic trick you can pull that will let you tiptoe around the policy and return your rancid DVD or game for the cash you so foolishly squandered, deflecting the supposedly hidebound policy back in the customer service desk's defenses like a light saber would a laser gun blast. Employing this Force requires no browbeating, smooth talking, or voodoo sacrifices—just a little bit of moxie and a resolve to keep a straight face.

Now that I've backed into the juicy stuff for a couple hundred words, here are the goods: Tell the man behind your desk that your disc is "defective" and "doesn't work," which is the whole truth in the metaphorical sense in the case of, say, *Kung Pow!* because it's a defectively-conceived film and the humor just doesn't work. Any reputable business will swap out your opened DVD for a fresh, unopened number directly off the rack.

At this point you may be shaking my book and screaming "So what? Now I've bought another copy of the same awful DVD. How does this help me in any way?"

Patience, my sinister-minded son. You're only halfway home.

True, you may have a copy of an awful DVD in one hand, but in your back pocket you'll still have the receipt from the original purchase. This document combined with your new DVD equals cash. If you want to be sneaky and prudent about it, you can just come back the next day and make the return, or you can be a hard-ass and just go for it in the same transaction. There's a decent chance you'll have to do some arguing to get your way, but relax—so long as you retain your composure and refuse to give in, you'll win because you're standing not only on the moral high ground but the legally firm position, too. All you need to do is have the manager read the part on the receipt that likely says, "Unopened discs may be returned within seven days" and you make him look like an ass in front of everyone in line. You'll be an instant intergalactic hero. Once your opponent gingerly hands you the receipt that says the purchase price has been credited back to your account, feel free to shout the "ZEEEOOOW!" sound of the light saber in an act of glorious domination. The geeks in line behind you will understand where you're coming from.

81. I Forgot My Wallet

There is no greater siphon of a man's funds—and thus no area with more potential savings—than a girlfriend. Especially cruel to the bottom line are the early, presex days of a relationship, when you're making like P. Diddy in order to impress the girl, showering her with nice dinners, expensive outings, and long, $20-cover-charge-filled, $10-drink-infested nights spent clubbing.

The simple way to mitigate all this nonsense, at least for one night, is to forget your wallet on an early date.

Now, now. Don't call me names just yet. I'm not talking about the cheesy eighties movie way of purposely forgetting your wallet and sticking a girl with the tab of an expensive meal. Sure, doing it that way may get you some free grub, but it will also likely damn your relationship, or at best, force you into the awkwardness of having to cut her a check the next day to make up for your malfeasance. Either way, you're guaranteeing yourself a sex-free evening.

The cool, classy time to announce you've forgotten your wallet is long before you've sat down for a meal. Make the declaration a few minutes after you've picked her up or met her up and exchanged niceties. Be sure to do so early, so as not to stick the lady with any unnecessary expenses, but not so early there's time for you to backtrack and go fetch it. The goal is not to siphon off your date's credit, but to reframe the parameters of your evening together. Dinner is probably now out of the question, meaning you'll fill the time by simply hanging out, maybe walking together or sitting outside a movie theater to gawk at and make fun of all the people. I'm not gonna lie, I got this one from the Steve Martin book/movie *Shopgirl*. See, even someone as rich as Steve Martin is still trying to think of ways to save money on dates.

Since you don't have your ID on you, drinking is out, that is unless she's willing to go back to your place with you, in which case you're already on easy street.

Play it right and you may even be able to extract a little romance out of the situation.

As you gulp in pretend embarrassment, dart your eyes about and check your pockets frantically to verify your oversight, make sure to produce with great relief a $20 bill or two you "accidentally" left in your jacket pocket just for emergencies. Now you can charm her with your creativity and upbeat nature, willing to make something sweet out of an adverse situation. With any luck you'll be able to make yourself appear so spontaneous and charming, it won't matter to her that you'll emerge from the night a little bit richer than you initially thought. You'll be that much closer to sex, that magical activity that drastically reduces the amount of money and activities you'll need to come up with, because in a sexually active relationship there's always something to do.

Warning: It should be a no-brainer that you can only use this one once per girl. The second time you forget your wallet you'll either be revealed as the con artist you are or an incompetent fool incapable of taking care of himself, let alone someone else.

82. Your Place or Yours?

Congratulations! Now you've slipped past the costly, early days of a relationship and have moved on to the pseudo move-in. You've got a set of clothes, a comb, and a toothbrush at each other's place. If one of you has a roommate and the other lives alone, it's obvious where you'll be spending the majority of your time. But if you both happen to live alone, you're presented with the opportunity of shaving percentage points off your heating and cooling bills. If you dwell in an extreme climate, such as the frozen Midwest or Northeast or the overheated Southwest, the cash you'll save on utilities will more than offset the extra gasoline it will take to be driving to her place constantly.

What I'm getting at here is it's better to spend as much time as possible at her place rather than yours. In the summers you'll be able to keep your air conditioning turned off, and in the winters you'll save on heating. Don't feel bad, because you won't be increasing her bills, just decreasing yours.

It doesn't take much to get this dynamic flowing—just a few compliments of her decorating style, how comfortable she's made her place, and how much nicer it is than yours. If your lady friend takes to coming over to your home more often than you'd like, be sure to fill your own apartment with more dirty dishes, clothes left on the floor, and utter swill than you normally would. Even more important, act the good guest when you're at her place, being careful to pick up after yourself so she has no reservations about having you over.

Not only are there financial benefits to being the traveling party in the relationship but creature comforts as well. First off, it's always nice to have your unkempt man cave to be used as a retreat during a fight, and it saves you the hassle of having to throw her out of your house. Second, there are disadvantages to being the waiter rather than the arriver. Offer to visit her and you won't need to be all dressed and ready to go, stuck at home waiting on your takes-forever-to-get-ready girlfriend to finish primping and finally mosey on over. When you're the one on the move, you've always got the natural excuse of bad traffic to account for the occasions your *World of Warcraft* raids stretch a tad longer than expected. Third, you don't want to suffer the indignity of having to explain to a friend why there's a box of tampons in your kitchen sink cabinet or hair ties wrapped around every doorknob. The emasculation of your living quarters will surely come one day, but you don't have to usher it in any sooner than need be.

83. Leave before the Encore

Now that you're practically living together, you can get away with a lot of things you couldn't before. You can relax your table manners, cleanliness standards, and restrictions on asshole comments that pop into your head. If you're a man at this advanced stage of a relationship with a woman in her mid-20s or beyond, the odds are great that she's already vetted you for marriage material and is giving her friends and mom biweekly updates on how close she senses you are to popping the question. This stage, which I refer to as the "tractor beam" portion of the romance, may seem panic-inducing, but it's not without its advantages. Basically at this point your woman won't dump you unless she catches you having sex with her sister on top of her favorite comforter while watching that Asian porn DVD you promised you threw away three months ago.

In short, behaving like a jackass every now and then won't torpedo your relationship.

Now think about how you can use this to save you some money. Is there a type of music she enjoys that you despise? For hypothetical purposes, maybe Christian music, country, *American Idol*–spawned pop artists or reunited boy bands? Does she like to attend the concerts of "artists" who perform this revolting brand of ear-splitting defecation?

If your answer to any of these questions is the affirmative, then sit down, lad, and let me enlighten you.

The next awful concert she invites you to, respond with all the enthusiasm you'd muster if she was asking you to join in a three-way with her old high school cheerleading teammate. Offer to buy the best seats available and have the tickets delivered to her with flowers. In the days leading up to the event, declare again and again how excited you are. Act giddy as you practically skip your way through the turnstiles.

Okay, bear with me here. What you've done at this point is build up her expectations to the point where she's convinced you won't act like a dick at this concert. Then once the music starts, you pull a 180 and behave like a bigger dick than that monstrosity Ron Jeremy packs.

Pull out all the stops and let yourself freestyle like Eminem in *8 Mile*. Crack jokes throughout about how awful the music is. For instance, if you're watching a male country star crooning a love song, insist that he wrote that song for a sheep. Scream, "When will this song end?" midway through. Moan, "I can't believe how much I paid to see this crap" over and over again.

Do you see where I'm going with all this? The point is to ensure you're never, ever, ever invited to one of these shenanigans again. You want to associate the idea of taking you along to one of the dopey concerts she likes with your bad behavior, sort of like what the government did to Malcolm McDowell with violent cinema in *A Clockwork Orange*. The fact that you were acting all nice before the concert will amplify the shock and awe of the misery you put her through at the concert to the point where she may stop enjoying this type of music altogether.

If the concert is nearing its end and you feel you haven't yet accomplished the goal, it's time to go Nagasaki. When the final set ends, bolt out of your seat and leave, even as the morons around you start clapping for an encore. When your date stays put and beckons you back, shoot her an angry glare and walk out in disgust, yelling, "I can't take any more of this music! I'm leaving," giving the impression that you're walking out on her.

Then glumly sidle back up to her, suffering through the infernal encore as she sops up her tears and you shake your head and chastise yourself for how immature and selfish you are.

Spend the drive home and the next several days apologizing profusely. You'll be hanging on by a thread at this point, but the thread will hold so long as you make sure not to snip it, because you love each other so much and this was just one road bump. Things will work out, and your life will be all the better for it.

A final note: My advice may sound specious, but I insist on its validity because I lived through the exact scenario with the woman to whom I'm now married. The very same woman who bore my children, and the very same woman who will give me a well-deserved bitch-slap for bringing this up again if she ever reads this book. In the interest of full disclosure I must say that I did not plan to get myself banned from all country music concerts with Jessica the night I took her to see Colin Raye, nor did I plan on threatening to abandon her before the encore. But my folly produced a fantastic result that I continue to appreciate to this day. I definitely stumbled onto something there.

84. The Legend of the Cubic Zirconium Heirloom

Of all the scams I've ever concocted, none fills me with the pride than the Zirconium Heirloom. I can announce with trembling pleasure that this idea is a pure stroke of unadulterated genius sent down to me directly from the highest heaven. In addition to its money-saving capabilities, it includes a component to advance social justice that will potentially save lives, and if adopted by a significant portion of the world population, may well destroy one of the most evil industries humanity has ever known. I'm confident that the benevolence of this advice will negate all the sinister stuff in this book and redeem my tainted soul. Everyone I've ever told about this idea of mine has instantly lavished me with near-worshipful praise. It really is something Gandhi, Einstein, or Mr. Wizard should have thought of first. My only regret is that the idea came to me too late in life to serve any personal benefit.

So here it is: When it's time to propose to that special lady with whom you'll spend the rest of your life, do so with a cheap cubic zirconium ring you picked up at a department store— Wal-Mart has got 'em cheap—and tell her the bauble you're slipping on her finger is a very special and priceless heirloom passed down through your lineage. Since a cubic zirconium rock looks exactly like a diamond, she'll never be the wiser unless she lets an appraiser take a look at it. If she does that, she's probably too materialistic and will likely spend you out of house and home anyway, so break off the engagement and save the ring for the next girl you decide to marry.

By pulling the Legend of the Cubic Zirconium Heirloom, you'll not only save at least a couple thousand dollars but you'll do your small part to improve the human condition.

A small primer for those who are confused at this point: Diamonds are one of the greatest frauds industry has ever pulled on the consumer, second only to the Catholic church's sale of plenary indulgences in the Middle Ages and the Abdominizer. The popular perception is that diamonds are among the most beautiful and rarest of stones, hence their extravagant price. In reality, diamonds are matched and exceeded in beauty by countless other natural stones, and close to exactly replicated by cubic zirconium, a synthesized scientific concoction. Diamonds only came into vogue in the last century, when the leading producers colluded to stifle supply and start a campaign to get celebrities to popularize the stones. You'd think driving the price up a thousand-fold would be enough for diamond manufac-turers, but you'd under-estimate their greed. To save on costs, they exploit miners in third world countries, forcing employees to work in unsafe, often slavelike situations for sweatshop-level pay. Even worse, the corporations fund violent dictatorships and militias in exchange for security and mineral rights, sometimes providing guns and ammunition for both sides of senseless wars in which innocent women and children are slaughtered, all so they can jack up the price of the engagement rings women have been brainwashed to desire since they were little girls by the media-marketing complex.

So please, if you're able, play into the white lie of the cubic zirconium heirloom tale and do your part to sling a rock at the diamond goliath.

I foresee a future utopia in which real-life grandmothers will knowingly pass down cubic zirconium heirlooms to their grandsons in order to fool the planet's dwindling population of diamond-obsessed wives-to-be. The diamond giants will crumble and the mines will collapse. Blood diamonds will be no more, and the stones will bear no more value than, say, cubic zirconium.

85. Preempt, Postpone Nuptials

Once you're sure the woman is the one you'd like to spend the rest of your life with—okay, once that girl you've been dating for years has finally broken you down completely and you're pretty sure you won't be able to find anyone hotter—it's time to get married. The process starts, of course, by presenting your prospective life partner with the zirconium heirloom engagement ring. The proposal triggers a countdown much like the digital numbers on LCD screens of bombs you see in action movies, only there's no red or blue wire to cut. You're doomed, my friend, and it's only a matter of how long you'll be able to postpone the inevitable. You'll be giving up your social, sexual, and financial freedoms, and friends, family, and especially your fiancée will expect you to mark this occasion with a solemn funeral to mark the end of your old life as you start your new one. And I whole-heartedly implore you to generate whatever remaining shreds of your decayed masculinity you can muster to make one final stand: Avoid the wedding at all costs.

When I say "all costs," by the way, I'm most definitely not speaking metaphorically. In 2005 a Fairchild Bridal Group survey estimated that the average American wedding costs $30,000. You don't have 30,000 ass hairs to your name, let alone dollars. And if you're not willing to pay for it, the bride-to-be's parents most likely will. This may seem like a good idea at the time, like a mobster who steps in and pays off your debt to a bookie, but don't fall for it. Letting your future in-laws pay for the festivities is a grave mistake, for they'll only do so to raise your interest rates, then bust your kneecaps when you can't pay them back. Er, that's what the gangster would do, actually. Your in-laws will be even crueler, lording the wedding cost over you for the rest of their lives as a token of your inadequacy. These people will have enough reasons to despise and be condescending to you—don't give them another.

Your eventual wife will try to ply you with guilt, insisting she's cultivated the fantasy of a big wedding since she was a little girl. Don't fall for it. When I was a little boy, I wanted to play for the 49ers. Some things don't work out. Deal.

It may seem as though everything is lined up against you. Even your own mom will nudge you toward a wedding. You'll look around and see a thousand bayonets all jabbing you in the ribs toward the hell of place settings, reception halls, and boutonnieres. But be sure to heed the words of the Rolling Stones. Time, most definitely, is on your side.

Don't forget that you've got a colossal bargaining chip at your disposal: You could care less if and when you ever officially tie the knot. She's got friends who are marrying left and right, engaging in a game of musical marriage chairs, and she's determined not to be the last one standing. Weddings are superfluous and a crass waste of money, and deep inside she knows it, and she's got none of her usual clout to shoot you down from her moral low ground. She can't even pull the "don't you love me?" card because you've already demonstrated your commitment by proposing.

Your goal in this situation is to wait so long to set a date that your better half must decide which she loves more: you or the idea of fulfilling her irrational wedding dream. You can't address the wedding situation head-on, because she'll hammer away at you until you give in. It's best to skirt around it; put it off. Change the subject. Say you can't talk right now. Delay, delay, delay. Whenever she pins you down and demands a straight answer, calmly tell her you'd gladly marry her this minute, but April 24 won't work because the Yankees are in town that weekend.

Wait long enough and she'll be so desperate to lose her eternally engaged rage stigma that she'll consent to rush off to the justice of the peace or go to Vegas to be married underwater by a skydiving Elvis at a drive-through chapel. Even if you happen to have had the $30,000 in savings all along, save it for a more worthwhile endeavor, such as a spin on the roulette wheel, before you bind yourself to marital bliss.

Full disclosure: Just like the zirconium thing, I didn't practice what I'm preaching here. I let her parents pay for the damn wedding.

86. Hold That Ejaculation

When Alexander Pope wrote, "Fools rush in where angels fear to tread," I'm pretty sure he was referring to your wife's vagina.

If that $30,000 figure from the last chapter rattled your ribs, let me toss another one out at you: $32,000. That's how much *Newsweek* estimates it costs to raise a kid in his first year.

Hold on, now. I'm not advocating never having children. Repopulating the human race is of such importance they dedicated an entire episode of *Battlestar Galactica* to the matter. Kids are great. I've got two kids and every second of their lives is priceless bliss.

And by "priceless" I mean "a hell of a lot cheaper than $32,000." Medical bills aside, I've probably spent less than $500 total on them. Why? Because I played it smart. I waited until three months after my little sister had popped out her first baby before I knocked up my wife. Thus little nephew Gabriel is a full year older than my Luke, and a full eight times more expensive. Also, we waited to have our second kid until we learned my sister-in-law was pregnant with a girl, creating a healthy seven-month gap between my niece Shelby and my daughter Emma, who is inheriting Shelby's clothes.

You see, everything my sister, sister-in-law, or anyone else for that matter, buys for Gabe, Luke eventually gets. Clothes, toys, swings, bouncers, bottles, everything. They gladly give us boxes of the junk, not so much out of benevolence but of the need to walk around their houses without tripping over the mutant baby clutter that fills every hallway and closet. They give us so much stuff that sometimes I feel bad and consider paying them for it, but then I stop and realize I'm doing them a favor, and besides, I didn't ask them to buy any of these things. They need me to take the hand-me-downs away or otherwise risk losing the little munchkins underneath the rubble of teddy bears, sleep-and-plays, and Bumbos. (A Bumbo is this totally awesome plastic thing that trains babies to sit up. You should totally inherit one from a sibling or friend with a slightly older kid). It's either give the old stuff to me or throw it away. Also, my sister honorably put her career on hold to look after Gabe for the first year, so bam! Instant free daycare. Well, I did pay her $100 a week but only to establish the precedent that she'd have to pay me if the situation was ever reversed.

I've found the seven-month-to-a-year gap between nephews/nieces and your own kids to be the ideal distance. It's just wide enough to keep a fresh, uninterrupted pipeline of freebies flowing, and not so distant my sister considers holding a yard sale. Hopefully others will benefit from a similar situation. If your wife is pushing quickly for a baby because her biological clock is ticking, tell her you'll buy her a new one for $32,000, and that you've got an erectile-dysfunction inducing headache until your best pal's wife pops out her first rugrat. There's no greater aphrodisiac than knowing your ability to keep it in your pants a year longer than your friend will save you $29,000.

87. AOL LOL

Should you be unfortunate enough to be still stuck in the landline and dial-up Internet zones in this advanced age, take solace in one pleasure: At least you don't have to pay for an ISP service. Sure, it may take four hours to download stuff, but you can rationalize the inconvenience in return to not getting anywhere from $40 to $70 jacked out of your checking account as a monthly sacrifice to the all-consuming pagan idol known as broadband.

Play it right and AOL will hook you up with free dial-up service for as long as you like. All you need to do is sign up for a free trial period, threaten to cancel when the account is about to expire, and then sit through a spiel from one of AOL's retention specialists, who will nearly always offer you another month or two in exchange for your willingness to hold off on bailing just yet.

You'll be taking advantage of the desperation of a wounded giant; a company with a colossal ego bruise willing to give you the shirt off its digital back in hopes you won't abandon it entirely. Already AOL dishes out two of its top features—its well-designed e-mail system and ubiquitous instant messaging application—for nothing. Longing for its turn-of-the-century hegemony, the AOL Internet service provider is hemorrhaging subscribers so quickly that employees are instructed not to take "I'd like to cancel, please" for an answer.

Some pitfalls to watch out for: If you lose track of your subscription date and fail to cancel before your trial period is over, you'll be billed for another month. To be safe, call a couple days ahead of your end date. Occasionally, when calling for your extension, you'll get a cowboy on the other end of the line who's onto your game and calls your bluff. In this instance, go through with the cancellation then set up a new account with a new screen name. You can still check your e-mail and IM with your old name, since those accounts are separate from your dial-up.

I enjoyed uninterrupted, free AOL from 1996 to 2005, when I was suckered in by Comcast's $29.99-a-month cable Internet trial rate. Once the cost rose to $45, I was already so addicted to lightning-fast por—I mean sports scores, yeah, sports scores, there was no way I could go back to dial-up. My efforts to pull the same scam on Comcast were met with indifference, so these days I'm a broken buck; a civilized full-rate-payer like everyone else. I long for the days when I had AOL eating from my hairy palm, and I'm envious of those who forge on with 56k modems and that denoo-denoo-gra-SCRAAAAGH—the sound of AOL coughing up yet another free Internet connection. The sound of victory.

88. Thanks but No Thanks

The social contract of the holiday and birthday gift exchange is a dumber, more futile idea than the San Diego Chargers's drafting of Ryan Leaf. We're all adults here, fully aware that there is no Boogie Man, Sasquatch, or WMDs in Iraq. And yet most of us cling to the notion that the things we secretly desire will magically appear before us, wrapped in bows, on birthdays, holidays, and anniversaries.

I can't speak for you, but when there's something I need, I go out and get it. In my experience the only people who don't behave this way are dopes who either drop heavy hints to gift-givers in their circle of what they're expecting or flat-out tell them what they want, as if they're ordering out of a catalog.

People like me don't want any presents and don't give gifters any advice or direction, and thus everything we receive needs to be returned for store credit that can be used to get something useful.

My advice to you here is to return absolutely every gift you ever get, be it an embarrassing sweater, a dollar-bin DVD, or a clay ashtray made by your seven-year-old girl at school. Those art teachers will drive a hard bargain, but usually they'll let you upgrade to a coffee mug or paperweight. In the case where gifts you've received just aren't returnable, such as a wristwatch from your dying grandfather, the standby of regifting is always acceptable.

Don't be ashamed of your all-return, all-the-time policy. In fact, go a step beyond nonshame and freely advertise it to everyone who inquires. When someone asks you how you're liking that Wal-Mart garden tool set, feel free to grin and state "Oh, I didn't need it so I returned it for a $16.25 gift card. Used it to fill half a tank of gas. Made my Sentra ride like a dream to work and back for four days!"

Hopefully others will come to recognize the futility of buying you anything, and thus stop expecting gifts in return. The only thing worse than getting a pointless gift is having to get a pointless gift for someone else. Once we all finally stop buying each other useless junk, we'll all be a lot happier. Our social socio-economic structure may collapse for lack of market stimulation, so we all may be unemployed and flung into another Depression, but it should be a happier Depression than the last one.

89. Cheapest Grocery Store, Laundromat, and Residence

It's a common misconception that after college it's no longer okay to mooch off your parents. Not so. Your mid- to late twenties is a prime time to oink with joy and snort your way through the parental slop trough. It's a matter of logistics: Your parents are now empty nesters or close to it, and now that you've got your degree in hand they no longer have to cough up tuition, so they're flush with cash. Meanwhile you're out in the real world making your start, and the sympathy angle is high because your folks will be able to see a little bit of themselves in you. This translates to an open-wallet policy if you need help with down payments on vehicles or houses. If you're lucky enough to have divorced parents, that means you can play one against the other, dropping hints to your dad that his ex must love you more since she and her new-and-improved money-bags trophy husband are hooking you up with a gift car rather than just offering to cosign on the loan.

The pleasures of utilizing your parents as extra

assets don't stop at cash. You can always fall back on the pro-totypical college routine, dropping by with a tub of laundry to clean and an empty backpack to fill in a pantry grub-grabbing spree. Even better, take it up a few notches by suggesting you miss your mom's home cooking and how great it would be if they start hosting a weekly dinner. Unless you're a Culkin, moms and pops will pounce on the suggestion like Brian Urlacher on a Matt Leinart fumble. These people, after all, haven't been able to relate to you since you were ten and now you're offering up hours of quality time on the cheap, validating their parental skills and bestowing them bragging rights at the office.

Once your weekly meal is on, you've just reduced your weekly dinner budget by nearly 15 percent, plus possibly a few more depending on whatever leftovers you haul back home. Again, for children of divorced parents, you're in an even more advanta-geous situation—double the figure to 30 percent.

Parents are also a valid excuse to not have to spring for cable TV. Whenever there's a big game or TV show on, you can make it ritual to pop in. If they've got a big DVD or book collection, they become your personal lending library.

Every so often you may begin to feel a twinge of guilt for taking advantage of your parents' generosity, but if you think it through, you'll find that the worries are unfounded. If you don't have a kid, imagine that you do. You'd give the child everything you could without a thought. By allowing your parents to do the same for you, you're doing them a favor. So really, by taking your parents money, food, and movie collection, you're actually putting them further in debt to you. And the way for them to repay is with their house.

That's why it's of utmost importance that you become a boomerang baby and move back in with your parents as soon as physically possible, and certainly before any of your siblings get the idea. True, should you retreat to the nest, you may suffer the stigma of being a thirty-five-year-old burnout who can't take care of himself, but you'll find that most of the time even your best and most candid friends won't make so much as a peep about your living situation. They'll probably feel too bad for you, unaware of your diabolical designs on the real estate and the inherent long-term-gain potential of the plan.

See, the goal is to inherit the house ahead of time without having to suffer through the pain of your parents' deaths. You will outlive them, especially if you stay away from chili cheese fries, and eventually outsiders will interpret the situation as your being a kindly, selfless man who cares for his feeble, geriatric parents rather than as a lecherous freeloader.

90. There's Only One Charity That Matters

When it comes to charity, my advice is the same as it is for tipping: Don't do it.

That's a rather blunt way of looking at the art of giving. A better way is to see it as giving generously to that one charity that matters most of all; the one destination you're absolutely sure your money will be put to positive use: yourself.

Most charity givers I've met get their high from giving to outside worthy causes. And that's fine. After all, dumping $20 a paycheck to the United Way and another $50 in the collection plate is a heck of a lot cheaper than buying coke. But the brutal truth is that cash you use to line your dealer's pocket is just as likely to be put to a worthwhile use as the money you're dumping into a charity. At least you know a street thug won't squander 80 percent of his take-home on administrative costs and overblown dinner galas that serve stale chicken and caviar to society types.

The fact is, all you charity givers, your piddling donation amounts to a miniscule portion of your chosen philanthropy's budget. Dish out 10 percent of your income for your entire working life to a big charity, and you're not even coming close to matching the organization's PR budget for a year. That's right— you're not even paying an organization enough to ask for other, big-money donors for their dough.

Lest you think I'm pulling this concept out of my ass, please visit Guidestar.org, a service that keeps track of tax forms for nonprofits. You'll be in for as much a shock as Neo was in *The Matrix* when Morpheus told him he was nothing more than a hallucinating robot battery. You'll find black-and-white evidence of a brutal world of six-figure-salaried organization honchos, outrageous office expenses, and, my favorite, fund-raisers that actually lose money. While some nonprofits are more efficient than others, and there are no doubt some truly needy and deserving causes, it's all a wash unless you're a millionaire because you really can't be of much help.

All the real charitable impact is provided by wealthy and corporate donations, most often as tax shields. If you want to do something nice for a charity, send Time Warner or Newscorp a letter asking them to send a donation to the organization. In comparison, your money is so worthless you may as well be donating Monopoly money.

Meanwhile, consider your lack of donating as a way of giving yourself a big raise for being awesome.

91. It's the Thought That Counts

You always hated the guy when you were a kid. He was the crazy, out-of-touch uncle who carved wooden toys from blocks of wood and gave them to you on your birthday. When you opened the presents and started to groan, your mom would pinch you in the ribs and you feigned excitement. The guy would smile sheepishly, and you'd respond with a glassy-eyed half-scowl. *Isn't this guy aware of He-Man, Thundercats, or Transformers?*

What you didn't learn until much later is that your uncle was crazy like the Grinch. He felt unjustly burdened by the annual gifts now required by his sister's offspring. *So the condom broke,* he reasoned, *why should I have to brave the madness of Toys R Us?* Your uncle refused and thought of a way around the folly, rightly reasoning that when you're absolutely required to give a present, homemade is the only way to go. Such gifts are invulnerable to criticism, and in fact demand overpraise from the receiver in order to make up for their disappointment, pretending to be touched by your tireless, crafty efforts. Even the time my uncle gave me a rattlesnake skin stuffed into a plastic bag, my mom exclaimed her joyous excitement and pinched me in the ribs until I did the same. Likewise with the time he gave me a wooden train set. Your uncle didn't care that no one played with wood or trains anymore, but he also knew you had to pretend you loved it.

Now that your sister has put you in the same situation your mom did your uncle, you've come to understand the wisdom of his demented ways. He knew that it's not the thought that counts but the appearance of the thought that counts. So what you need to do is head on over to a craft store, troll the aisle for a $2 toy car, then mash on it with a butter knife, dulling the corners and chipping off the finish, until it looks sufficiently awful to the point where your sibling will believe it was really you who made it.

Homemade gifts also come in handy for your spouse. Notice I said "spouse" and not "girlfriend," because you probably want to wait until regular sex has left your relationship in order to forge on with this plan, lest booty be withheld as punishment for your cheapness. Also, when you're not yet married, it's still possible to actually give each other things. Married people, on the other hand, go through a charade of pretending to buy each other stuff, refusing to recognize the reality that it's impossible for two people who share the same pot of money to buy each other something. Something ceases to be a gift when it's your joint checking account that pays for the purchase.

It may make you feel sneaky to buy your wife a gold necklace and watch her eyes light up, while inside you know that her paycheck contributed to half the cost. If this is your mind-set, slap yourself in the face until you realize that you still had to pay for half of it, and why are you spending that kind of money to impress someone you've already conquered into the yoke of marriage? Sure, you used to have to romance her through such ridiculous methods, but you've moved long past that stage, as has she. Think, does she give you blow jobs or laugh at your jokes anymore?

My favorite spousal gift solution is the coupon book. Grab some construction paper and a pen, fold it in half to make it a book, then fill each page with various offers of things you wouldn't normally do, such as "One Free Foot Rub Anytime," "I'll Cook Dinner and Wash the Dishes," or "This Voucher Will Stop Me From Watching Any Football Game." She'll be charmed that you're willing to do so much for her, then forget about the coupon book and never take you up on any of what you promised. Just like that, you've gotten more spousal credit than three gold necklaces and haven't had to spend any money or effort.

92. A Friend in Need

There's a heartfelt and valuable lesson at the end of the movie *It's a Wonderful Life*. After Jimmy Stewart decides not to kill himself, he returns home where his friends shower him with money so he can save his family's bank and keep him from going to jail for embezzlement. The message is that it pays to have friends.

The challenge is in finding ways to get those friends to pay off before you've stooped to Jimmy's situation. The solution is to prey on their insecurities.

Encourage your pals to take financial risks you'd never dream of and you'll be rolling in perks that would make Jimmy Stewart rise from the grave to shake his fist in jealousy. If you've got a pal who makes a lot more money than you, mention how cool it would be to own a time-share in Hawaii, but that "guys like you and me" could never afford it. Your friend, offended that you would dare to lump your sorry, minimum-wage ass with his hard-earned bourgeoisie aesthetic, will respond with the natural instinct to prove he can afford your suggestion. Now that your friend owns a Hawaii time-share, you own the time-share, only you don't have to pay. He'll probably even suggest you tag along on a getaway just so he can feel as though he's lording it over you.

The same method works for just about any material possession you desire: cars, ATVs, video-game systems, DVDs, CDs, and power tools.

Your undue influence can also inspire friends to stick their neck out and break the law for a situation that could benefit you both. For instance, say you'd like to continue downloading songs illegally, but you're afraid you'll get sued by Metallica. If your friend has a big enough ego and/or needs to impress you, he'll offer to download whatever songs you need for you. This can also work with movies. You'll both possess the lawbreaking material, but should the record labels or studios come after anyone, it most definitely won't be you.

It's also a great idea to talk up the awesomeness of black boxes—the contraptions that splice into your cable line and allow you access to all the channels and pay-per-view movies for free. These are great ways to see all the porn, UFC, and Wrestlemania events you desire without having to pay the exorbitant fees. If your buddy doesn't bite, you might want to buy one for him as a "gift." He'll be elated, unaware that you're secretly aiming to benefit from the black box's benefits without having to expose yourself to any of the risk. Your pal will be so grateful, he'll gladly let you take advantage of the luxury by letting you invite yourself to his place as often as you like.

93. Garage Catalog

While it may be intrinsic to human nature to regard those who live around you with fear and contempt and avoid talking to them under any circumstance, abiding by this tendency is a foolhardy and costly measure. Get out there and meet those who live around you, because otherwise you'll never know how they can be of use to you. A wise Spanish teacher once said, "Su casa es mi casa," or at least that's the way I remember it. Your greatest assets are the properties that border you directly because of all the goods and services available for no cost. Think of the dwellers adjacent to you as the Mexico to your United States given the following analogies:

EXPLOIT FREE TRADE AGREEMENTS: The United States imports Mexican goods on the cheap, and in return dumps the things it doesn't need much onto its trade partner, which is forced to accept them because there are no trade barrier tariffs. Consider your neighbor's garage as a catalog of wondrous goods from which you can purloin at will. There's no need to buy a rake, hedge trimmer, weed whacker, or riding mower when

Henderson next door already has the stuff. You can even "give back" as well, by handing him bag after bag of useless lemons that fall from your backyard tree. An odd thing about lemons—they grow so frequently and no one ever wants them, and yet neighborly bags of lemons just ooze with goodwill. They also provide appropriately playful ribbing in case you ever happen to break something of your neighbor's and pretend it was broken before you borrowed it: "Hey, man, here's a lemon, just like that busted cordless drill you let me use the other day!" Seriously, you can make it funny if you try. It's all in the delivery.

BENEFIT FROM FREE ILLEGAL LABOR: A neighborly favor, much like a request on a Sicilian man's daughter's wedding day according to *The Godfather*, cannot be denied. It's an established man law that a guy who sees his neighbor taking on a big project, say, painting, shoveling gravel, or laying sod, it's required to drop whatever you're doing and lend a hand. Once the extra hand is onboard your ship of foolish do-it-yourselfery, he's instant free labor. Hotel owners and meatpacking-plant managers would be envious. Should you slave away on some enormous task without drawing any help, you have the right to hint your way by knocking on the door with a seemingly unrelated query, such as picking up the newspaper for them so no one steals it or politely asking if what you're doing is making too much noise. The best-case scenario is when the wife answers the door. She'll notice the sweat on your brow and scream, "Harold, why don't you go help him shovel dirt in 100-degree weather?" I recommend moving in next to a big Mormon or Catholic family whenever possible. Both faiths instill deep guilt into their followers, and the typically large families often require stay-at-home moms, who can provide free day care.

HOLD DIPLOMATIC EXPOSITIONS: Just as American sports leagues such as NASCAR, Major League Baseball, and the NFL hold spectacular events down in Mexico to offer as goodwill gestures (but really just to spread the penetration of the cultural empire), it's always a great idea to get your neighbor involved in whatever Fourth of July potluck or Super Bowl party you've got going. If they're invited to your shindig, that gives you the automatic right to use their entire driveway and street front for overflow parking, as well as hit them up to cohost the thing with you and split the food costs. If your neighbor has a bigger backyard, better grill, or fancier TV, you can suggest moving it to his place, shifting the majority of the burden out of your territory and onto foreign soil. Block parties are even more fun when you don't have to clean up.

94. Now Boarding for the Departed

It's a problem frequent travelers face all the time: I've just decided that I really want to go to Miami and hang out at the beach, but I live in Idaho and I want to be there tomorrow and not have to wait the two weeks to get the discounted fare. The answer: Pretend you're going to a funeral and beg the airline to cut you a break on the ticket price.

An urban myth goes that airlines no longer offer cheaper rates to people who need to attend long-distance funerals. These "bereavement rates," which can slash up to half off the price, are still in effect, however. The misconception is that since they aren't posted on Web sites or spelled out in brochures they must not exist. You can't blame airlines for not advertising this policy, for fear of being taken advantage of by shameless shysters like you and me. In fact, I'd hazard a guess that it's the airlines themselves that propagate the misconception that bereavement rates are no longer in effect, spreading the word in a secret viral campaign in order to banish the idea of the discount from consumers' consciousness.

Many airlines even have a pilot's wives club that donates air travel miles toward the cause. All you need to do is call and ask for the discount, then submit yourself to a minor grill-session meant to snake out the cheap fraud-mongers. All you need to do to keep hope alive is stick with a somber tone and maintain an airtight story of your fictionally deceased relative. It also doesn't hurt to scan the obituaries section of the newspaper at your destination in order to add to the authenticity factor. As is the case with most negotiations, uncontrollable sobbing is also a huge plus. Remember, on the other end of the line are real people, not computers, so you want to emotionally pander as much as possible. Once you claim your boarding pass at check-in, it's a nice touch to wear black and don sunglasses.

Don't let your conscience get the best of you and prevent you from going through with it. Sure, it's possible airlines have a set quota of discounted bereavement trips they bestow each year and you may well be taking one from someone who has a genuine funeral to get to, but think of it this way: Anyone who is truly devastated over a death probably won't pause to think, "How can I save some money on this deal?" so the only people you're screwing are tightwads who aren't exactly crestfallen over their loss, and probably don't really need to be going to the funeral as much as you need to go to Miami on vacation.

95. Milking It for All It's Worth

This little tip won't save you all that much money, and it seems excruciatingly disgusting the more I think about it, but what the hell. It served me well back in my starving college days, and I'd be remiss not to share it.

My advice has to do with cereal, and how to make milk last longer. This invention spawned from the necessity of living in a dorm freshman year that was located several miles from the nearest grocery store. I've always been a cereal killer in the morning time, so in order to feed my habit I had to buy my milk from vending machines that were constantly running out and restocked only once a week. I came to treasure my half-pint milk cartons and did everything I could to make them last. I'd stow them in the back of the miniscule box refrigerator I shared with my roommate, barricaded behind the corroded pizza slices and half-eaten burritos to prevent shareage. And when I finished eating my bowl of Marshmallow Mateys each morning, I'd funnel the excess milk back into the carton. By doing this I could make a tiny portion of milk stretch far beyond its due date. And as the days went by, the milk tasted better and better, more sugary and mallow-riffic. By the time I was tapping the final drops out of the carton, the liquid was approximately 90 percent sugar-based and oh-so-tasty. I often have nostalgia for the taste of my two-week-old sugar milk; now that I'm so wealthy I no longer need to recycle my dairy products.

An appendix: Some may call me out right here for being a fancy lad who ignorantly decided he had to have milk with his cereal like some rich kid. "What's wrong with munching it dry?" they might ask, or "Why not eat cereal with water as your lubricant instead of milk?"

My answer to these queries is, "Well I'm a snob when it comes to how I like my Apple Jacks, dammit." Man was not meant to eat his cereal with water, which dissolves the sugar in cereal and sogs it up too quickly as opposed to the way milk fills out the (un)natural flavors of your beloved boxed product and gives you at least fifteen minutes of crunchiness before it penetrates the outer shell of your Rice Krispies. I'd sooner skip a meal than compromise it with water.

Also, I reserve the dry munch for snack purposes only. Unmilked cereal is a lot like cookie dough—it seems like a great idea at the time but after a couple mouthfuls you wonder what you've gotten yourself into and you feel a little sick afterwards.

96. The Can-Can . . . Can

I've always wondered why there's such a big push to recycle aluminum cans. Is our soda container supply really running so low that it's necessary to have waste management companies collect little bins full of recyclable cans to everyone in civilized society?

No matter. The fact is this is a gravy train waiting to be hijacked by whatever desperado is up to the task. All those Diet Coke cans are tin gold, I tells ya. And it would bring a tear to my eye to see so many saps just toss them into the garbage or dump them into the recycling bin for free if I didn't recognize the personal benefit to such waste. If you catch my drift, I'm advising you to troll your neighborhood on can pickup day, rifle through everyone's bins, and hustle them on down to a pay center, where you can nab anywhere from 4 to 10 cents per can. All you need is a plastic garbage bag. Once you fill a bag and take it home, it's a good idea to use a mallet or your foot to stomp the cans into discs that don't take up as much space. You can also pound them into your forehead if you don't mind losing IQ points through repeated brain trauma.

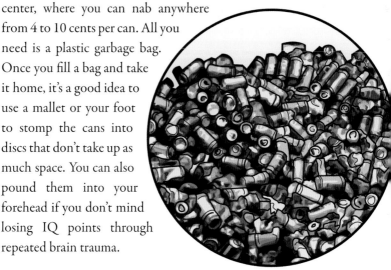

Other easy ways to collect cans include bringing a box to your office and labeling it "recycle soft drink cans." As long as you take the goods home regularly, it's doubtful management will get in your way as long as you clean out the box regularly. Trash cans outside of grocery stores are also easy pickings, thanks to their common proximity to vending machines.

To those who would say collecting cans is beneath them, I say look at the numbers. The aluminum industry pays out $800 million every year to crazy, money-grubbing can collectors, and you'd be a fool not to pick up on some of that action. The money comes to you for little effort, and it's tax free. Sure, there's a downside: Can-collecting tends to leave you with sticky fingers and a sunburn, and if you leave them in your garage too long you'll attract ants, but you'll be surprised how fun and addictive it is to hunt for the cans regardless. There's a certain sense of pride in strolling down the street with a colossal bag full of cans hoisted over your back. Don't do this near a city park, however, lest you want to be confronted by a shiv-wielding homeless man desperate for your bounty.

Another idea to make recycling work for you is to zip behind Wal-Marts and Targets to collect the corrugated cardboard they toss out, then turn the stuff into cardboard manufacturers for as much as $80 a bale. The stuff isn't as easy to lug around as cans, though. I've never tried collecting cardboard, but I have friends who swear by it. These friends own extended-bed trucks, though, and I do not, so I restrict my recycling adventures to items I can carry in a bag.

97. Lose Weight in Your Gut, Gain It in Your Wallet

Allow me to take you back to August 1996. I was a young lad fresh out of high school, unable to land a job at the *Daily Wildcat*, the University of Arizona campus newspaper. My roommate Josh and I decided we needed jobs, so we filled out a general student union application at 10 AM our first day on campus and were pleased to be offered instant gigs, working at the Chick-Fil-A. We'd start that same day at noon. We giddily accepted.

Josh wisely backed out and stayed home, but I thought I'd give it a try. Ten hours later, I quit when my shift ended and told Josh I'd decided I'd rather not have any money than work in fast food. Josh nodded solemnly and shared with me a great secret that has served me well through my years.

Take a can of tuna, add a few squirts of steak sauce, and slap the result in between two slices of bread and you've got a culinary masterwork that will satisfy your hunger and cause the flab to slip off your belly.

At first I scoffed at the notion—steak sauce is for steak, not tuna!—but after one bite I was forever hooked. This was far better than the pickle-egg-and-mayo tuna salad I had grown up with, and so much cheaper and easier to make. I now had a lunch and dinner staple to go along with my breakfast of cereal and recycled milk.

Eating A1 and tuna sandwiches daily my freshman year of college allowed me to get by on less than $10 a week, and I shed twenty-five pounds off my already wiry frame. Each time I came home to visit my parents, they told me how gaunt and lifeless I looked and asked if I needed any money. I laughed off the silly offer, content that I was pulling one over on the world by surviving without a job or parental assistance. I'm probably lucky I didn't die of scurvy, though.

98. Hostel Takeover

Most cheap travelers know that crashing in hostels is the least expensive way to get a night's rest without resorting to elbowing bums off park benches or camping in creepy rest areas filled with serial killers and rapists. The smelly, piss-stained beds and cardboard-thin walls are well worth enduring in return for more money to waste at the Amsterdam hash bars and red-light district.

Only the supercheap, however, know how to save even more money off the nightly hostel charge. Take advantage of the hostel's old-timey ghettoness and you'll have a free place to stay as long as you stick to the same area for an extended period of time.

To pull this off, check into a hostel that uses actual keys—none of this newfangled magnetic strip card nonsense. Make a copy of the key, then check out of your room each morning and re-up for a new room shortly afterward. After a few nights, you'll have nearly as many keys as the crusty old manager and will be able to slip in and out of rooms as often as you desire. When you're freeloading, be sure to check in as late as possible, when foot traffic has died down and the manager has fallen asleep at his desk. Once you're inside a room, never leave your door ajar and do your best to hide all evidence that you're inside. Also don't be surprised if drunken revelers barge into your room in the middle of the night. Keep your bags well-packed for a quick exit, then leap out of bed and depart with a nod, making for the nearest room for which you have a key.

By the way, never try this in strange Eastern European countries with improbably hot girls looking to tempt you into a night of kidnapping and torture for hire at the behest of ruthless wealthy locals who pay to see Americans' dangling dislocated eyeballs severed with scissors. Since it happened in Eli Roth's *Hostel* flicks, I have to believe it also happens in real life, and I don't want to be held responsible to one-eyed readers coming after me for bloody vengeance.

99. Memory Mate

You'll never have memory problems again if you hit up electronics stores in just the right way.

Sure, you could go the usual route and spring the $15–$20 minimum to purchase a memory unit, or you can be dishonest and manipulative and get as many as you'd like for free. By that untrustworthy look on your face I can already tell which way you want to go.

If you're in need for a smallish memory card, buy a digital camera or video-game machine, then pull out the memory stick and return it the next day. Usually the dude at the counter won't even open the box, but sometimes he'll run a check, spot the missing memory stick, and question you. If he goes this far, just say one of the reasons you're returning the item is because it's missing the memory card. Take care not to go too far and insist the "missing" piece isn't the only reason you're returning the camera, otherwise they may ask to replace it with the same item. Of course, you can always shake this request off if you insist you've already purchased another one at a different store.

You can do this as many times, in as many electronics stores you can find. I'd advise hitting up each store no more than once to avoid suspicion. You can keep the cards for yourself or unload your goods at online auctions for instant return on your nothing investment. The only drawback is that the packed-in memory sticks are usually pretty skimpy. Sell enough, however, and you'll be able to afford something of decent size. Too bad the same isn't true for your, uh, undersized appendages.

100. Craigslist Clairvoyant

Benjamin Franklin is often quoted as saying, "A penny saved is a penny earned," but what the history books won't tell you is that the quote was edited for brevity. The full text went on to read, "But six thousand pennies earned by convincing some dope online that you're a psychic are priceless."

Or something like that.

My pseudonymous friend Nina Lang did just that to earn money before she became a professional journalist. Her tale of triumph nearly brought a tear to my eye. I'll let Nina's advice, printed here with my permission, speak for itself:

> I'd post an ad that basically said I had this special ability and felt compelled to use it to help people. Then, when they contacted me, I cited personal safety concerns (it was craigslist, after all), regarding why I felt more comfortable using e-mail. Sometimes I lied and said that distance helped me do more accurate readings—basically, I was lazy and didn't want to come out and meet strangers, and I also wondered if I'd feel comfortable scamming people to their face.
>
> I would charge $30 for a two-page reading and $60 for a ten-page reading. Sometimes people would get really into it and send me personal effects by mail, like envelopes from the people they wanted a reading about. I encouraged them to ask questions, and it'd always be what you'd think: Is the boyfriend cheating on me? Will I ever find love? I'm not happy at my job and what should I do? It really ended up being lots more psychotherapy than "prediction"—it

doesn't take a psychic to know that if you've seen her car in his driveway three times this week, yes, he's probably seeing her again, and it doesn't take a clairvoyant to say, "If what you're doing feels wrong, look inside your heart and see what it tells you."

So, mostly the "readings" would be about 50 percent practical, situational advice couched in esoteric talk, 25 percent universally applicable compliments (making the individual feel good increases their likelihood of believing what you're telling them), 20 percent totally vague future predictions, and 5 percent very specific ones.

With the specific ones, if you're wrong, they'll forgive you, because it's only 5 percent of the reading, and if you're right, they'll keep relying on you forever, because, y'know, you were *so* specific!

The weird thing is I was often right with the specific things, just random stuff I pulled out my ass would turn out to happen, and I'd get e-mails at midnight just begging for me to do new readings immediately. Like I said, I never got a lot of clients actually buy into the "e-mail reading" thing, but those who did were loyal repeaters. I might have made about $500 that way one summer while I was on unemployment.

And in the end, I really did help people—either by giving them legit reasons to believe in themselves, or by providing some harmless emotional support, so I didn't feel too bad about it. Whenever I started to feel some guilt about being a "fake psychic," I thought, "Wait a sec—do I really believe there's such a thing as a *real* psychic? At least I'm honest!"

The buried epilogue to this inspiring saga is that I got her to write all that by penning a simple e-mail that read, "Hey, have you ever pulled a money-making scam?" And off she went, monologuing like some sort of James Bond villain, dutifully writing part of my book for me while cheerfully getting nothing in return. Bless you, Nina Lang.

Acknowledgments

Above all, thanks to my agent, Neil Salkind, who sold what almost every one of his colleagues deemed impossible to sell. Thanks to editors Bill Wolfsthal, Julie Matysik, and everyone at Skyhorse Publishing who took a chance on me and were so generous and helpful at every stage of production.

Thanks to everyone who read this manuscript at various stages of editing, especially Tom Kirlin, who may be the only person on the planet who comes up with sketchier money-saving ideas than I do, as well as Leigh Alexander, for placing a close second to Tom. Also thanks to Meghann Marco, who helped steer me through the publishing world, Adam Chromy, who taught me how to write a book proposal, and Jeff Schmidt, who was encouraging.

Thanks to my wife, Jessica, and kids, Luke and Emma, for giving me reasons to love life. Thanks to my parents, Ross and Cindy, for their love, encouragement, and free meals every Sunday night that continue to this day. Thanks to my sisters, Linda and Laura, for being awesome friends to grow up with. And thank you to my grandparents, Howard and Frances Strayer, whose library inspired me to become a writer.

I appreciate the help of all the editors I've worked with at the *Arizona Daily Star*, in particular: Kathy Allen, B. J. Bartlett, Josh Beach, Tom Beal, James Bennett, Bobbie Jo Buel, Cathy Burch, Ann Brown, Rodney Campbell, Shannon Conner, Kristen Cook, Mary Cooney, Dave Eubank, Teri Hayt, Dennis Joyce, Debbie

Kornmiller, Norma Coile, Anne-Eve Pedersen, Brian Pedersen, Tim Konski, Diane Luber, Theoden Janes, Inger Sandal, Tom Heleba, John Humenik, Chuck Kramer, Maria Parham, Dave Ord, Nick Pintozzi, Dave Skog, Sid Steketee, Scott Simonson, Scot Skinner, Jill Jorden Spitz, Jason Stallman, Myles Standish, Yui Umehara-Garewal, Raina Wagner, and Randy Wright.